Coping Skills Therapy for Managing Chronic and Terminal Illness

Kenneth Sharoff, Ph.D., has been practicing psychotherapy for thirty years and is currently in private practice in the Phoenix, Maryland, area. He received his B.A. from the University of Colorado, his M.A. from the University of Denver, and his Ph.D. from the University of Maryland. He is the originator of cognitive coping therapy, reviewed as "the most important contribution in the development and maturing of cognitive behavior therapy in the past twenty years." He is the author of *Cognitive Coping Therapy* and lives in Baltimore with his wife and two children.

Coping Skills Therapy for Managing Chronic and Terminal Illness

Kenneth Sharoff, PhD

Springer Publishing Company

Springer Publishing Company, Inc.
536 Broadway
New York, NY 10012-3955

Acquisitions Editor: Sheri W. Sussman
Production Editor: Sally Ahearn
Cover design by Joanne Honigman

03 04 05 06 07 / 5 4 3 2 1

Library of Congress Cataloging-in-Publication Data

Sharoff, Kenneth.
   Coping skills therapy for managing chronic and terminal illness / by Kenneth Sharoff.
      p. ; cm.
   Includes bibliographical references and index.
   ISBN 0-8261-2275-2
   1. Cognitive therapy. 2. Adjustment (Psychology) 3. Chronic diseases—Psychological aspects. 4. Terminal illness—Psychological aspects. 5. Terminally ill—Psychology. I. Title.
      [DNLM: 1. Cognitive Therapy—methods. 2. Adaptation, Psychological. 3. Chronic Disease—psychology. 4. Critical Illness—psychology. WM 425.5.C6 S531c 2004]
   RC489.C63S533 2004
   616.89'142—dc22   2003067289

Printed in the United States of America by Integrated Book Technology.

This book is dedicated to my mother,
Betty, a truly loving and giving person.

Contents

Part I

Coping Skills in Health Care

Chapter 1

Coping Skills Approach

This book rests on the basic premise that people feel good about themselves, function well in the world, and have fewer interpersonal and intrapersonal problems when they know how to cope. Coping requires skills, which provide an "organized response to a situation with the purpose of attaining a goal or resolving a problem" (Sharoff, 2002, p. 2). Coping skills reduce the burden that stressful life events impose on people (Snyder and Dinoff, 1999). They allow people to combat whatever stressor is affecting them on even terms and not be overwhelmed by it.

With disease onset, a repertoire of skills must be in place to manage the disjuncture from the old way of living, the diminution of life satisfaction, the intimidation of discomfort and pain, the specter of disability and death, and the adulteration of identity. Abilities need to be in place to cope with the upsurge in stress that threatens mental stability. Chronic or terminally ill patients may falter if those coping skills are not in place.

The biggest problem for medical patients is that normal living has not prepared them for the multiple demands imposed by disease and treatment. They have to face unique situations, problems for which they have no prior training or talents. They have not had the time nor background to face the many challenges put before them by an infirm, crippled, or dying body.

The purpose of this book is to provide a broad range of skills to face the hurdles medical patients must overcome in order to avoid dissolution. This book is about how to cope with conditions no one wants but must deal with and provide the tools: cognitive, emotional, perceptual, physical, and behavioral abilities. This book will demonstrate to chronic and terminally ill patients how to get what they need, by revealing *how* to succeed. (Throughout the book the term "medical patient" is used for either a chronic or terminally ill patient.)

Sharoff (2004) has written a companion book for this text entitled, *Coping Skills Manual for Treating Chronic and Terminal Illness.* (This text is referred to in this book as "the manual.") It provides assessment tools, guidelines for treatment, and techniques for addressing resistance, difficult patients, loss of identity, and other problems. Included in the manual is a computer disc that contains questionnaires for assessment and handouts for patients to develop various coping skills. (The symbol *** will be seen throughout this book to indicate that it is a handout on the disc.)

ASSUMPTIONS OF COPING SKILLS THERAPY

A coping skills approach makes several assumptions about pathology and dysfunction in medical patients:

1) Symptoms of psychopathology in medical patients (e.g., bitterness, physical discomfort) develop not so much from the disease or treatment for it but by the patient's inability to cope with the disease or the treatment for it. The struggling medical patient is the skill-deficient medical patient.

2) The nonpathological population is not symptomatic because they have sufficient coping ability. Medical patients' emotional problems will recede or disappear when they learn how to cope with their problems.

3) The trauma of being a chronic or terminally ill patient is not caused by the disease as much as the inability to cope with the chronic or terminal illness. Because of that, the traumatized patient has to confront ill health, disability, or death ill-prepared for what lies ahead. This in turn can worsen the course of disease.

4) Medical patients feel vulnerable not nearly so much because of the disease and its effects as the inability to cope with being vulnerable.

5) Disease and treatment invariably cause some degree of suffering, discomfort, bitterness, deprivation, helplessness, uncertainty, and rejection of the patient, but if appropriate coping abilities are present, these problems or situations will cause less harm and far less psychological pain.

6) The feeling of being out-of-control is real. Appropriate coping skills enable medical patients to regain or retain control of their life in a situation that diminishes control (e.g., disease, treatment side effects, treatment requirements).

The coping skills described herein provide structure and allow the patient's sense of strength and self-confidence to prevail when there are life-altering conditions, such as chronic and terminal illness.

BENEFITS OF BOOK AND MODEL

This book advances an approach—the coping skills method—that was developed for the medical patient. Most of the coping skills that have been developed are for psychological problems, such as a lack of social skills, lack of assertiveness, or continuing stress. These skills show patients how to remedy a problem. However, medical patients face many problems that cannot be remedied, such as chronic pain, physical disability, erratic health where symptoms come and go, or progressive deterioration that slowly sucks functioning from everyday existence and finally the ending of life. They have negative emotions that recur again and again that cannot be avoided, such as frustration, suffering, helplessness, guilt, and rejection. For these difficulties, they need a different group of skills not previously discussed in the literature, skills that teach acceptance, allowance, tolerance, and accommodation.

Medical patients even without preexisting psychological problems are also forced to face formidable, daunting, or disheartening situations. To deal with those situations, combinations of coping skills and tactics are required different from what is needed for managing ordinary troublesome situations. This book details those skills along with how to present them to patients.

Coping skills can be attained in various ways. They can come into existence naturally and in that case they are genetic. They can be learned through operant conditioning, when particular behaviors are either rewarded or punished. Skills can be learned from watching others and that is referred to as social learning (Bandura, 1969). People can also create their own skills by using their creativity and intellect.

However, the skills medical patients need to possess are not taught. Normal prior learning does not address the unique problems that they will face. Genetic predisposition may not arm patients with the abilities needed for adjustment. Because of that, tools are needed to teach medical patients how to navigate through unknown waters. The author hopes to fill that gap.

The book also provides tactics for dealing with different types of diseases, because they vary so much from one another. Each disease type requires a distinctive coping skills repertoire to overcome the problems unique to that disease. For example, the problems in dealing with asymptomatic disease differ from progressive, deteriorating, non-terminal illness, remitting/relapsing conditions, or stable disabling conditions.

Many coping skills appear quite simple, but on closer examination they are actually quite complex. Many coping skills are comprised of *chains of subskills* and those subskills are comprised of other skills that can be called *microskills*. Too often health providers do not know how to reveal the intricacies of coping. They pass on such wisdom as:

- "This is something you will have to live with. Try to adjust."
- "Relax and don't get so stressed. Don't worry about this so much."
- "You will have to tough it out."

Yet, these same providers fail to illustrate the specific steps to carry out such general advice. They do not reveal the subskills and microskills that patients must successfully master in order to follow the provider's recommendations. Without that detailed information, patients may appear to be noncompliant or resistant. The author seeks to overcome this problem by detailing the links in the chain of coping skills and illustrating what skills are required to build others, or how to mix and match skills to accomplish different goals.

The chaining of skills is accomplished by a *master skill* to form a general coping ability. The master skill is a metacognitive ability, to think about what to think to accomplish a goal. The master skill is an ability to arrange and select subskills and microskills to accomplish a particular strategy. However, frequently a patient's master skill needs to be developed further or s/he is unaware of what skills need to be positioned in the coping skills chain in order to achieve a desired outcome. We will attempt to refine and train the master skill in medical patients, so they can run their own lives in a more efficient way.

Further, the book brings together a range of approaches from other practice models. It intertwines such diverse models as cognitive restructuring (Ellis, 1962, 1971, 1998; Beck et al., 1979, 1990; Salkovskis, 1996), paradoxical therapy (Haley, 1973; O'Hanlon, 1987; 1989, Weeks and L'Abate, 1982; Watzlawick et al., 1974), solutions oriented therapy (Selekman, 1999; deShazer, 1985, 1988, 1991), Gestalt (Perls et al., 1951; Polsters, 1973; Zinker, 1977), self-management therapies (Rehm and Rokhe, 1988), and behavioral therapy (Bandura, 1969). These models provide therapists with a broad range of choices to accomplish treatment goals.

A coping skills model in general offers many advantages for health care. This is a highly practical, level-headed approach: a person has problem X; provide a tool to fix problem X. The model may be used readily by every health-care professional: doctor, nurse, occupational or physical therapist, and, of course, mental health therapist or counselor. The provider does not require vast training before s/he can readily use this model. It immediately can be put into effect in any setting, in an outpatient or inpatient facility, any long-term care unit, or even an emergency room.

It is a perfect approach for the nurse or medical social worker who has only a short period to work with a patient before he is discharged from the hospital. This model is harmonious with managed care because it works quickly and efficiently in brief therapy. Because the approach is so problem-focused, a provider with a coping skills package can address a single issue in just one session!

It is also most helpful for providers who cannot meet with patients on a regular basis, due to time constraints or a busy practice. Because the model has the patient monitor and evaluate a skill's effectiveness, providers can teach a set of skills, assign them as homework, and then assess its efficacy weeks or even months later.

Patients like this model, too, because it turns the provider into an expert on how to resolve problems. Patients come to providers wanting both information and a prescription that can ease their pain or distress. They want the provider to guide them in overcoming their plight. The coping skills therapist operates that way. S/he is a highly active participant in the process and takes on such diverse roles as teacher, director, organizational consultant, inspirational mentor, and of course counselor.

COGNITIVE COPING THERAPY

Coping skills therapy has been around for many years, providing educationally based, single skills for specific situations (D'Zurilla and Goldfried, 1971; Goldfried, 1980). However, it had not developed into more than a "loose, heterogeneous collection of skills, a grab bag or patchwork of techniques" (Sharoff, 2002, p. 1). It was mostly known by a few dominant skills such as relaxation training, problem solving therapy, social skills training, and assertiveness training. It lacked a coherent practice theory and was used more as an adjunct to other treatment models to resolve specific problems such as stress, passivity, or social ineptitude.

Yet, using ingenuity, this is a model that can be greatly expanded to include many, many more skills. The approach could have become a mainline method of treatment, but that has not occurred. Addressing the lack of development of the model, a new approach has come along in the last year called cognitive coping therapy (CCT) (Sharoff, 2002). It has greatly expanded the number of coping skills, provided a cohesive practice theory, and a theory of pathology and health. Here, cognitive coping therapy will be extended into the medical arena to show its usage with chronic and terminal illness patients.

COGNITIVE-BEHAVIORAL THERAPY

Coping skills therapy is part of cognitive-behavioral therapy (CBT), a method of care that has received significant support in research and practice. It has been referred to as a "paradigm revolution (Mahoney, 1974) because it dramatically changed the focus of treatment from early childhood events and behavior to cognition. CBT also includes cognitive restructuring (CR), which in actuality is the dominant approach in this model. In most people's minds, CR is CBT. Cognitive restructuring approaches, such as Rational-Emotive-Behavioral Therapy (REBT) (Ellis and MacLaren, 1998) and cognitive therapy (Beck et al., 1979) do use coping skills as part of their work, but it is secondary to the belief change method discussed below.

CR focuses on the central role of thinking in human functioning and its influence on the emotional, physical, and behavioral response. Its primary emphasis is on how thinking mediates between stimulus and response. After the activating event has been explicated, along with the response to the event, the belief about the activating event is identified. That belief is scrutinized to determine if it is rational and realistic. Rational is defined as a thought that "aids and abets people achieving their basic goals and purposes" (Dryden and Ellis, 1988, p. 217).

To help patients assess the benefit of their thinking, CR asks them not to take their thoughts for granted as a fact. Instead, the thought is converted into a hypothesis and tested for validity. The intent is to determine if assumptions, inferences, and interpretations are accurate, if they are supported by facts. Patients are also asked to identify alternative meanings in addition to their own definition of the situation, alternative consequences besides their own prediction about what will happen in the future, and alternative causal beliefs and beyond their own idea about what caused something to occur. The reason is to make people question their own thinking and entertain other perceptions of reality, in the mission to find the truth. Ellis (Ellis and Harper, 1975) believes that there are core irrational beliefs shared by most people that are at the root of mental health problems. These thoughts are questioned, to see if they are upheld under cross-examination. Ellis (1971) refers to this as disputation. If a belief fails to be upheld as rational and realistic then patients are invited to change their belief so it better reflects the facts in the situation, or to adopt a thought that is more reasonable, prudent, or pragmatic. Finally, CR seeks to verify if the new thought leads to goal attainment.

While CR addresses the content of thinking, the main reason people end up with difficulties is because of their degree of confidence in a belief. A high degree of confidence in a thought is termed certainistic thinking by CCT (Sharoff, 2002). Certainistic thinking is a major problem when there is not supporting empirical evidence for a belief but an individual nevertheless maintains that idea is correct. With certainistic thinking, a closed feedback loop exists and there isn't a search for supporting data. The intention is to create an open feedback system where facts and other's input can be heard and reviewed without bias. Various techniques have been developed (Beck et al., 1979; Wesslers, 1980; McMullin, 1986) to challenge certainistic thinking.

In addition to structures of thought, another problem lies in the process of thinking. There are cognitive tendencies in information processing that distort the perception of the situation. They are referred to as cognitive distortions (Beck et al., 1979; Burns, 1980; Dryden and Ellis, 1988).

The above description represents the rationalist school of CR in CBT. It asserts that cognition is the prime mover in adjustment. They propose a linear model where beliefs have a causal supremacy over emotion or behavior. There is also a constructivist model that proposes reciprocal causality between them (Mahoney, 1988). See Sharoff (2002) for discussion about CCT and each of these perspectives.

CR works on the idea that pathology can be corrected by changing erroneous thinking. CCT also works to change erroneous thinking, but not directly. It will either give patients appropriate thoughts that are part of a coping skill, or inculcate a coping skills package that indirectly changes patient thinking. Like CR, CCT makes cognition a central part of its treatment.

THE COGNITIVE FOUNDATION OF CCT

CCT works with three types of beliefs that shape the development of coping skills. They are policy beliefs, executive beliefs, and operational beliefs. Each plays a different role.

Policy Beliefs

People set policy for their lives by making fundamental plans for how they want to live. They plot courses of action for themselves based on others, institutions, and higher powers such as God, fate, or lady luck. They promulgate guidelines for behavior and responses to events, proscribe how events should proceed, how the world should be, and what treatment they can expect from others. For instance, they set principles for what providers should do for them in case of illness, what should happen to loved ones if they are no longer present, or how an employer should act in case of their illness. A policy belief is not a specific and detailed protocol or design, but a general guideline. They often appear as standards or absolutistic beliefs, a want, or an expectation (Sharoff, 2002). In general, cognitive restructuring focuses on policy beliefs. It maintains that beliefs—functioning in the form of policy—are the primary reason for patient problems.

A policy belief comes to the fore when any event occurs. A position must be taken, so the current policy on that subject is reviewed. If no policy has been developed, then one is formulated regarding how to address that event. The policy belief has an influence when formulating specific directions for how the self needs to respond to the event. However, there are many ways to carry out or execute the policy and matters of execution are separate from policy decisions. Two people may have the same policy but have vastly divergent ways of realizing that policy.

The following are common examples of policy beliefs regarding health, disease, and treatment. The main policy is given first and usually leads to a secondary policy that is an outgrowth of that position.

- My body should not interfere with my ability to pursue my career. Secondary policy: No disease should interfere with my career advancement. I will not tolerate my disease plaguing my job.
- I will tolerate being sick for a short period of time, as long as it does not go on too long. I will determine what is 'too long.'
  Secondary policy: I will not tolerate a chronic illness when it goes on too long. I will know when enough is enough.
- I must be available for my children and do what is needed so they get their needs met. Completing my role duties as a parent is vital. Secondary policy: A disease should not interfere with my role duties as a parent. I must not inconvenience or put burdens on my children before they are ready to assume them.

- I will stick with my spouse even if he becomes sick.
  Secondary policy: He should do the same for me now that I have become sick. I would not reject him if he became ill, so he should not reject me now that I am ill.
- Looking good is vital. My body should meet my expectations for how I want it to look.
  Secondary policy: I cannot bear how this disease makes my body look.
- I should not be kept waiting if I have an appointment, because I am an important person.
  Secondary policy: No doctor should keep me waiting for too long. I will determine what is 'too long.'
- Doctors must find a cure for my disease. Doctors and modern medicine should be able to cure me.
  Secondary policy: I will find someone somewhere who can cure this disease. I am not ready to die (or be disabled).
- My retirement should be free of hassles and disappointments.
  Secondary policy: My disease cannot interfere with my retirement plans. The treatment for this disease should not make me feel ill.
- I will see my son graduate from college before I die.
  Secondary policy: I am willing to die after he graduates.

In the above examples, the policy beliefs determine what the body, other people, doctors, life, or God must do or not do. The policy claims rights (e.g., a retirement free of hassles) for the individual and gives permission for certain actions (e.g., I'm willing to die after he graduates). Notice how they are an attempt to control bodily processes and other forces that are essentially beyond the individual. They position the person at the center of the universe, which is basically irrational thinking. Ellis (1973) has stated that people do this to overcome their own powerlessness and inconsequential position in the universe. It is a response to the existential dilemma of trying to gain control of life in a world that is unconcerned with the individual.

With regard to treatment, providers need to identify a patient's policy belief regarding a situation, and then declare that the patient has set a policy. People do not realize and need to understand that their response is influenced to some degree by policies that they have made. Below are examples of ways to discuss policy with patients. Note how the statements indirectly link the policy belief to the patient's response.

a. You are quite upset that your husband has rejected you after you became sick. Does your husband have a right to do so? Do you have a policy about him staying with you if you become ill?

b. You have had many disappointments since you became ill and this has gotten you down. Do you have any personal guidelines for how many disappointments you can have in your life at any one time?

c. You're very angry about how your life has changed since you started treatment. Did you have a course of action in your mind about how treatment should proceed and how fast you could heal?

d. What were your expectations about how your treatment would affect you? You seem to have a preset idea about how much of a problem your treatment will present to you and your family.

e. You cannot do what the other kids in school can do because of your disease. How do you think your body could be compared with other students?

f. You had to quit work since your heart attack. I hear how much this has depressed you. Prior to becoming sick, did you have a plan about when you would quit work? What was your idea about how your career would proceed?

Executive Beliefs

While the policy belief declares the plan or principle for a situation, it does not stipulate the exact response. CCT explicitly assumes that people form a more detailed, specific set of self-instructions and beliefs called executive beliefs (Sharoff, 2002). *Executive beliefs detail how to carry out the policy.* They specify the content of thinking, focus of perception, and if an emotion can be felt and expressed and to what degree, and which behaviors can be useful in a given situation. They instruct the person on how to manage his or her emotional response. They influence what actions need to be taken to attain a goal. They decide how and when a person should respond, and where that response may occur. They give permissions and prohibitions regarding that response for what is allowed or disallowed. In total, *executive beliefs circumscribe the exact* **response to the activating event.** They are a template or mental program that orchestrates being-in-the-world. Like policy beliefs, they usually operate on a semi-conscious level and out of personal awareness, but they can be consciously drafted. They are a metacognition because they provide the thought about what and how to think.

CCT explicitly assumes that executive beliefs play a more important role in developing psychopathology and emotional distress than policy beliefs. Because of that, it places far more emphasis on changing executive beliefs and inculcating new ones. To make this point, let us study the case of Sally.

Sally felt bitter after she became sick. That was due in part to her policy belief regarding physicians: 'Doctors should cure my pain and heal my body.' That policy was violated—in Sally's mind—when her doctor did not cure her. He was supposed to be a rescuer and savior but he failed. She continued being symptomatic and that infuriated her. Her irrational policy belief laid the groundwork for those feelings.

However, once she felt angry, Sally was then faced with how to cope with her emotions. She had to formulate a strategy about how to cope since her policy belief had been frustrated. Executive beliefs were then formulated to accomplish those tasks. What were they?

1. Mentally focus on my disappointment on not being cured. (This self-instruction caused her to remain fixated on a negative outcome instead of turning her attention to other matters that could lead to a more positive feeling.)
2. Blame the doctor for letting me down. (This self-instruction stems from an unrealistic attribution where he is held responsible for her continuing symptoms.)
3. She allows herself to vent anger at the doctor mentally. Lambaste him mentally because he let me down. (This instruction provides a vehicle for the anger by encouraging hypercritical behavior and intensifies Sally's anger first stimulated by the policy belief.)
4. Stay in the struggle to find a cure somehow.

This last self-instruction encourages Sally to combat the disease and try to overcome it. It turns her into a fighter to get her way. This is termed an *agonistic activity*, where someone combats another force and will not surrender the fight. This self-instruction plays a major role in why Sally becomes so upset when no cure is found, because she resents being defeated in her battle to beat disease.

Self-instructions 1–4 are part of a revenge-seeking coping strategy that features mental castigation of the supposed wrongdoer. On the one hand this strategy provided her with a way to cope by venting pent-up anger. She gained satisfaction by putting down the person who had disappointed her. On the other hand, the strategy is maladaptive because it only adds to her bitterness by highlighting how the doctor did not help. It encouraged mental ranting against him because of his supposed incompetence, leaving her more tense and bitter.

In summary, Sally's executive beliefs—not her policy belief— primarily drove her internal response. The executive beliefs were largely responsible for perpetuating her anger. While Sally has an irrational, unrealistic policy belief, that in and of itself does not have to lead to a problematic outcome. A patient can have that same irrational policy belief but a positive outcome, providing there are different executive beliefs.

For instance, Sally could have executive beliefs for handling her anger and disappointment with her doctor that are part of an optimistic coping strategy. Compare the self-instructions below to the revenge-seeking coping strategy discussed above.

1. Limit the mental focus to positive matters. Negative matters (e.g. the doctor's failure to help) should be ignored. (This self-instruction would allow Sally to overlook how the doctor did not help.)
2. Imagine a possible positive outcome in the long run. Try to find ways a positive outcome can be realized. (This instruction increases hope.)
3. Find a bright side of the negative situation.
4. Resist critical behavior and blaming.
5. If blaming does occur, do it in a mild manner. Overzealous, critical blaming will only lead to a pessimistic outlook.

With these executive beliefs, Sally's anger and disappointment with her physician should be minimal. She would not be intensifying her anger already stimulated by her irrational policy belief. In fact, there are several other adaptive coping strategies that Sally might employ, such as frustration tolerance (see Chapter 5), disappointment accommodation (see Chapter 9), or helplessness tolerance (see Chapter 12). Any of these strategies can avoid negative repercussions stemming from her irrational, unrealistic policy belief. The point is that *the virulent effects of a policy belief can largely be circumvented with the aid of an adaptive coping response.*

To further make the point that executive beliefs are the prime contributor to negative emotion, as well as the primary way to avoid developing negative emotions, let us return to Sally. However angry she was with her doctor, she continued to see him hoping that he would eventually provide relief from her symptoms. While she castigated him mentally, she had a policy belief that inhibited her anger. It helped determine how she would act with him: "I must get approval from significant people who come into my life, especially important people."

Ellis has called the above belief an absolutistic thought and has labeled it irrational. He cites it as a prime cause of emotional problems (Ellis and Harper, 1975; Dryden and Ellis, 1988). Does that have to be the case? In actuality, Sally's executive beliefs were largely responsible for *how* she tried to get his approval. They shaped her exact response on multiple levels:

a. Disallow any sign of bitterness while with the doctor. Don't be impolite when he comes into the room. Look cheerful. Stay civil. (This self-instruction rules out any expression of disappointment and forces her to suppress her feelings while with him, resulting in tension.)

b. Allow feelings of bitterness but do not express them in communication.

c. Play down any disappointment with the doctor when he asks how things are. Make the doctor feel good about himself. (This self-instruction makes the doctor's feelings more important than the patient's. It circumscribes what might be said to the doctor and how to interact with him.)

d. Keep focused on the doctor's face. Watch for any sign that he is displeased for not progressing under his care. (This instruction structures perception to be involved with the doctor and not her own emotions. Sally ignores and doesn't express her own frustration.

e. Don't be assertive with this doctor. Stay passive and do what he says. (This self-instruction sets the coping strategy of non-assertive behavior.)

Overall, Sally had a set of self-instructions for being a people-pleaser. Her executive beliefs designated how she would carry out her irrational policy belief. They compelled her to be non-assertive and solicitous. They denied her the opportunity to express herself, which may have made her feel better. They resulted in significant internal tension. Moreover, with no outlet for her anger besides mental castigation, her anger turned to bitterness.

However, another set of executive beliefs for the same irrational policy belief could have led to different results. While changing her policy belief is advisable, it could have been preserved without causing problems. She could have adopted an assertiveness-coping response while still believing that she must please others. Below are the executive beliefs for an assertiveness strategy.

1. Avoid getting the doctor angry by not being denunciatory or pushy.
2. Tell him that the treatment is not helping but in a friendly, soft, calm manner.
3. Praise the doctor's efforts and express appreciation for his trying to help.
4. Use fundamentals of assertiveness, such as making "I" statements ("I feel discouraged.") while avoiding blaming statements such as "You are not helping me."

Hence, while an irrational policy belief does cause problems the fallout can be minimal if a productive coping response is in operation. To use a statistical explanation, Sally's executive beliefs contributed to a larger part of the variance in regard to her emotions than policy beliefs.

In working with executive beliefs, therapists need to discover the response pattern to the activating event on multiple levels. This can be accomplished by posing such questions as:

- "What do you usually do when someone does X?"
- "What do you focus on when Y (or you) does X? Do you keep the focus on X or allow yourself to focus on other matters?"
- "How do you feel emotionally when someone does X?"
- "How intense do you feel when someone does X?"

The responses to these questions are then reconceptualized as self-instructions: "So you seem to tell yourself to do the following when Y does that behavior," or "It appears that you have chosen to tell yourself that it is okay to feel Z when Y does that action." The next step is evaluating the pros and cons, the benefits and limitations, of following a particular set of self-instructions. If patients continue to use a maladaptive coping response, then they now clearly understand the negative consequences from pursuing their strategy. By illuminating the self-instructions, patients have to take responsibility for their behavioral and emotional responses.

Operational Beliefs

Executive beliefs guide or inspire other thoughts that help to fulfill the coping skills strategy. They are termed operational beliefs, because they operationalize the self-instructions. Operational beliefs are the content of thinking. They are the content for communication with other people and are usually not questioned because they *seem* plausible, mostly because the executive beliefs have authorized them as a person's right or have given permission for them. Once a right or permission is in place, the person is guided or inspired to think in a particular way. Here is an example of operational beliefs and reveals how they are an outgrowth of both policy and executive beliefs.

Cognitive Formation of a Rejection of Suffering Strategy

Policy belief: Disease should not be so unpleasant.
                 I reject further suffering in my life.

Executive belief (EB):   Focus on the ill effects of the disease.
Operational belief (OB):   It's terrible how my life is now.
                           It's not fair that this has happened to me.

EB: I have the right to express my displeasure about how my life is going.
OB: "Things have really gotten bad for me. I am just miserable."

EB: Get out the anger toward the body for not healing.
OB: I am so disgusted with myself. I look like hell in the morning. I am so tired of how things are going. My body is just not responding to treatment.

EB: I have a right to express my anger at anyone who is causing me further suffering. I consider anyone increasing my suffering as my enemy.
OB: Leave me alone. Stop bothering me. Are you blind? Can't you see I feel rotten?

In reviewing these self-instructions, the interplay between policy, executive, and operational beliefs are revealed. The executive beliefs are developed to provide a rationale for rejecting further suffering. The individual sets the policy and then needs to execute that policy. But the execution cannot take place unless there is support for the policy. The self-instructions build that support by maintaining a focus on the ill effects of the disease. The person also needs to give him/ herself permission to reject further suffering and allowance to complain about having to suffer. This is facilitated by the executive beliefs that there is a right to express displeasure about the disease and voice criticism at anyone who might increase the level of suffering.

The policy beliefs are irrational and unrealistic. Setting a limit on how unpleasant a disease can be and rejecting suffering are not rational thoughts. This stimulates anger and displeasure. But, to make the point again, the policy beliefs contribute only partly to the emotional response. The executive beliefs are mostly responsible for the anger and displeasure experienced with others. They do not encourage coping responses that can lead to adaptation, but in fact encourage responses that will lead to more conflict in the medical patient's life. The same *irrational policy beliefs could stay in effect and there would be minimal frustration and suffering providing that a different set of executive beliefs were in operation.*

Below are examples of another set of self-instructions for the same policy belief that will lead to less emotional suffering:

a.   Even though I reject further suffering, I must accept it into my life.
b.   I must face reality and bear up under it; the suffering will not go away.
c.   Even though I don't want others to add to my suffering, I must be tolerant of them.
d.   If I don't want more unpleasantness in my life, I must forgive others when they upset me. That will make my life less unpleasant.

(These self-instructions are for an assimilation of suffering coping response, which is discussed at length in chapter 4.)

This author is not suggesting that therapists ignore irrational, unrealistic policy beliefs. They must be discussed because they do contribute to medical patients' problems. The book is only making the point that the major emphasis should be on executive beliefs—the self-instructions for how to live. CCT emphasizes replacing maladaptive, irrational executive beliefs with adaptive, rational self-instructions, and believes that is the primary treatment task.

Summary

This book maintains that medical patients will manage their disease much better with the aid of coping skills. It fills a gap in the literature by clearly spelling out the coping skills needed for chronic and terminal illness. The coping skills model is part of cognitive–behavioral therapy, which in the past has made cognitive restructuring the dominant approach in this model. However, CCT has been developed to show how coping skills can play a major role in health care. CCT focuses on: a) beliefs that set the policy for a situation, b) self-instructions termed executive beliefs that structure response, and c) thoughts (operational beliefs) that are given to others. CCT maintains executive beliefs are most important.

Strategies and Skills

This chapter deals with how people try to manage in general, and how chronic and terminally ill patients in particular manage their disease and its effect on them. It focuses on coping strategies or the broad plan for how to respond. When disease causes life changes and reduces life satisfaction, patients need to develop a strategy that can allow them to resume premorbid functioning. A way is sought to secure objectives and become reinvolved with the pursuit of goals. Strategies are formed for this purpose to take command and plan to combat problematic, difficult situations. In essence, the strategy oversees a type of combat operation, the resistance to the many life changes brought by disease.

People will always form strategies for coping. They may not cope in the best of ways, but they will nevertheless plot ways to get what they want. That is part of basic human nature. Once the strategy is formulated, tactics for accomplishing the strategy are formulated. These tactics require skills. The master skill that we all have appropriates the necessary skills to fulfill the strategy. The master skill puts together a combination of faculties to allow the strategy to succeed. After selecting appropriate skills, it positions them to work in league with one another.

There is an intimate connection between strategy and skills. Strategies are formed with intent. Skills are the way to fulfill an intention and secure the objective designated by the strategy. The strategy maneuvers the person in various ways to achieve what is wanted while opposing whatever is interfering with goal attainment.

A skill used in one strategy can be reappropriated by another strategy and recombined with other skills to accomplish another goal. Skills are merely parts of the whole. Any part can be taken apart and put into another whole (another general coping ability). Hence, we can say that *skills are innocent but strategies are not.* Skills are merely tools and strategies are the plan for using the tools. Strategies are formed from previous life experiences and reflect those experiences. In the mind of a patient they are a way to attain a goal. The patient's strategy may not be the most adaptive way of operating or the best way to proceed objectively. *A strategy can be maladaptive in the long run or even irrational.* However, it is still that person's way of getting his/her needs met. See manual for a list of maladaptive coping strategies and how to treat them.

STRATEGIES, POLICY, AND SKILLS

Strategies interface with policy beliefs. They are a way to fulfill the policy, but they can also influence the development of new policy, Strategies can arise from an emotional response such as sadness or anger, or from a belief about a situation. They help form the executive beliefs.

To illustrate how strategies interplay with each other, we will examine the problem of helplessness. Raymond, a medical patient, feels helpless to control his life due to the effects of his disease. He has always had a strong need to be in control of his surroundings and whatever happened to him. He forms a strategy to cope with helplessness while at the same time developing his policy regarding the problem of helplessness. After forming his coping strategy, he plots his executive beliefs—mostly on an unconscious level—that flesh out the strategy. The executive beliefs become the vehicle to move the strategy along by providing the means to accomplish the strategy and the policy.

In this example, two sets of executive beliefs are compared. Raymond habitually selects executive beliefs A, but in therapy he learned executive beliefs B. A is maladaptive and irrational while B is adaptive and rational. The two sets of executive beliefs are provided for readers to show how the same strategy and policy can be achieved in two different ways but with dramatically different results.

Strategy: "Maintain control as much as possible. I will find ways to limit being helpless. I will limit losing control as much as possible."

Policy belief: "Helplessness is not allowable. I must gain control in some way to avoid it."

Executive beliefs A

1) Become angry when helpless. It is permissible to rant and rave at this time.
    Operating belief: "I am so sick and tired of being sick and tired."

2) Show my helplessness to others so they will want to rush in and take care of me. Act pitiable. Gain others' sympathy.
   Physical tactic: Raymond looks forlorn and miserable around his wife and doctor.

3) Comfort myself by thinking about how hard my life has become since becoming ill. Stay focused on my problems.
   Operating belief: "Things just never work out for me. Just my luck to get sick. Why me? It's not fair."

Executive beliefs B

1) Control what can be controlled. Accept what cannot be controlled.
   Operating belief: "I cannot control possible side effects from my medication. I will not get upset about this though and will control my own responses to those side effects."

2) Find areas where there is control and build on that. Tune into other things that are positive. Don't fixate on areas where I am helpless.

3) Enjoy those areas where there is control and savor them.

4) Don't emphasize areas where there is a lack of control; de-elevate them so they are not so important.

5) Practice *anger management skills* when feeling helpless so as not to lose control of my emotions.
   Operating belief: Easy does it. I can handle this.

Why would someone select executive beliefs A rather than B? What makes someone gravitate to one way of operating versus another? One reason is personality and early life experiences. Another reason is core, deep level beliefs called schemas and basic assumptions (Beck et al., 1979). A third reason is overlearned, deeply ingrained patterns that have been reinforced repeatedly over time.

Each therapist has to decide his or her area of focus. CCT maintains that early life experience, core cognition, or reinforced behavior does not have to control choice of coping strategy. Patients can adopt new adaptive, efficacious coping skills without examining their early life or changing their schemas. In time, use of those coping skills will alter the influence of early life experiences and change schemas. Sharoff (2002) has given several case studies to make this point.

Let us now examine the tactics in executive beliefs A and B, and the options open to Raymond. Executive belief A offers Raymond three tactics to limit further helplessness and gain control. First, he can use *angry protest (A1)*, where he complains about his life in the hope that someone (e.g., God, health providers) will do something about his plight. Second, he can use *impression management (A2)*, where he tries to create an image of himself as a hapless, down-and-out person to gain pity from a powerful other in the hope of getting help. Three, he can use *self-pity* to comfort himself when feeling helpless (A3). Strategy A is basically nonutilitarian (although many patients do practice that approach to situations) because it increases negative emotions and does not adapt to the exigencies of disease.

A second option open to Raymond is changing his policy belief. It is essentially irrational and unrealistic because disease inevitably leads to a loss of control over the body and goal attainment to some extent. Maintaining that policy will result in increased anger and frustration because a demand is made not to permit helplessness, but helplessness cannot be avoided. With such a policy in place along with executive belief set A, Raymond will not accomplish his strategy of limiting further loss of control. He will have more negative emotion that must be controlled, but he lacks tools to manage those feelings and is at risk for feeling out of control at that time.

The second option would involve restructuring the policy belief to be, "Helplessness will come with disease and that has to be accepted." Changing the policy to be rational and realistic will facilitate an "accepting" response, which will ease anger and frustration and avoid a backlash when helplessness is encountered. (Note: a simple change in policy belief will not in and of itself lead to acceptance. It will need to be supplemented by many other self-instructions and tactics to become a viable coping response.)

A third option open to Raymond is keeping the policy belief in operation but supplementing it with a set of rational, adaptive executive beliefs. The skills used in this effort will satisfy the policy belief that Raymond must stay in control. Strategy B provides for that by helping him control his life and avoid helplessness as much as possible. It works to bolster a feeling of being in control, by focusing on situations where he has influence and can control his emotions.

Why would this therapeutic strategy be utilized? Why not just change the policy belief, using cognitive restructuring? There are two reasons. One reason is that a change in coping skills and executive beliefs will yield better results in the long run. The patient will avoid self-pity that can lead to depression, increase life satisfaction over all, and increase his control over his emotions, which is what the patient wants most of all. A second reason is that many patients will resist changing a policy belief because they prefer operating in a certain way. Specifically, in the case of Raymond, he has a high need for control and steadfastly wants to remain that way. He has a rigid personality and feels vulnerable when his control decreases. CCT would work to help him maintain that coping strategy, by showing him how to be a better "control freak." That way he can preserve his personality with minimum negative repercussions.

Herein lies one of the strengths of CCT as a method of treatment. It is a flexible model because it is not wedded to one practice methodology. With one patient it may work to counter irrational policy beliefs and with another patient it may work to change coping strategies and skills. The decision about how to proceed is based on what the patient wants, and not what the therapist wants as a consequence of his/her philosophy of treatment.

There is also a fourth option not addressed so far: change the coping strategy altogether. The strategy of fighting to stay in control is often maladaptive in medical situations that limit considerably the patient's degree of control. Instead, a better strategy may be *accommodation to and tolerance of helplessness*. When a strategy is changed, the policy belief will also change. CCT maintains that people will be willing to change a policy belief once they realize that a coping strategy is impractical or maladaptive.

ASSUMPTIONS ABOUT SKILLS AND STRATEGIES

1)   *There is no such thing as a bad coping skill.*
A skill is only bad as part of a particular strategy. If another strategy can use that same skill for a different purpose, then that skill is appropriate. Further, if a strategy uses a skill to excess, in the wrong context, wrong time, or wrong sequence, then it is bad. The problem is not with the skill but how it is used, when it is used, and where it is used. That falls under the strategy, which decides such matters.

For example, denial can be used as a coping skill to avoid facing reality. Denial is chosen subconsciously and is an inappropriate skill when symptoms first appear. In the incipient phase of disease, patients need to know the full dimensions and repercussions of the problem at hand to make the best medical decisions. Similarly, terminal illness patients should not deny reality when first learning about their condition. They need to face reality to perform important tasks such as deciding how to live the balance of their lives in a meaningful way and preparing loved ones for their death. However, in the right context denial can be helpful. For instance, once terminally ill patients have realistically dealt with their future death, denial can be practiced, allowing them to believe that their last days will not be painful or that their departure will not devastate their loved ones. This will allow them to feel more comfortable making plans and facing death without extensive dread and worry.

2) *Maladaptive strategies, psychopathology, and psychological symptoms contain invaluable skills.*
When coming into contact with a patient's maladaptive strategy, therapists often fail to make use of the skills contained in that strategy. They focus on psychopathology and brand the actions that form the pathology "sick." By doing so, therapists do not look carefully at the viable skills developed by each pathology. These are resources that patients bring to treatment. CCT promotes an impartial viewing of maladaptive strategies and psychopathology.

Contained within any maladaptive strategy or psychopathology are invaluable skills that can aid adaptation and accomplish life goals. The treatment task is to use what the patient brings to therapy, and that means finding the positive within the negative, the wheat within the chaff. So often skills are overlooked or criticized by therapists because they are used in a maladaptive or incorrect manner. However, if they are readapted and redeployed, then they can be useful. The positive aspects of a maladaptive strategy can be combined with new skills as part of another coping strategy to form an appropriate response.

3) *Any skill has value if used in the proper amount.*
Some people can have a deficient or excessive amount of a skill and for that reason suffer or have difficulty adjusting to problematic circumstances. However, with an appropriate amount and use of a skill beneficial results are gained.

For example, the skill of self-attentiveness entails viewing oneself as an object not in only the mirror but also in the mind's eye, to assess if the self is maintaining an elevated standard regarding appearance. It is the ability to maintain a consistent self-focus and constant self-object in a variety of circumstances, as part of an overall self-caring strategy. However, self-attentiveness can also become a problem when used excessively, as in the case of a narcissistic personality. For instance, during illness, appearance can change dramatically for the worse. Then excessive self-attentiveness can result in a preoccupation with appearance, overconcern with self, and self-rebuke for not meeting a preconceived standard of beauty.

A second example makes the point that entitlement thinking in the right amount can be most beneficial. It can spur patients to assert themselves with doctors and other providers who are not giving appropriate service or enough information. It can be helpful to people pleasers who have problems declining requests or demands for services. It will rally patients feeling rejected by others to fight for a better life, because "I deserve more." Overall, entitlement is an important way to sustain self-caring—only when there is a proper amount.

However, an excessive amount of entitlement thinking causes problems. Patients in the health care system are just one of many and have to wait their turn. An excess of entitlement thinking can result in difficulty adjusting to waiting time. It can spur patients to demand special consideration and care, causing relationship conflicts with doctors or health care staff. Excessive entitlement thinking can even cause an irrational, fanciful demand for a cure or exemption from illness, because of beliefs such as "I should not be dying because I am a special person," or "I should have a better and more rewarding life, not the life of a disabled person." Because of excessive entitlement thinking, patients become more vulnerable to dejection and disappointment, when they do not receive what they demand.

4)   *Irrational, unrealistic policy beliefs, and maladaptive executive beliefs do not necessarily have to be eradicated. Both can be supplemented or repositioned for another context, and so that they may become viable.*
Part of the job of coping skills therapists is rewriting policy and executive beliefs when necessary, to make them more adaptive. One rewrite job is adding on to a policy belief. Many policy beliefs can offer helpful guidelines for the future providing they are not the only guidelines operating. For instance, an anxious medical patient frightened about proceeding with new treatment or surgery will often have a policy belief, "Be cautious and avoid vulnerability at all costs." This policy is helpful in some contexts but may cause problems in other contexts; for instance, when a patient avoids a needed medical intervention because it poses some risk. Hence, a policy can be carried too far. In that case, it needs to be supplemented with another policy, "In certain circumstances be bold and take risks." Hence, a new policy of *cautious boldness* can be promoted with anxious patients. When put into use, it can allow a patient to proceed into the unknown, but with prudence and careful consideration.

Likewise, the executive beliefs that play out the policy belief to "be cautious and avoid vulnerability at all costs" also have to be supplemented. For instance, anxious patients have a self-instruction to focus perception on any sign of trouble and to steadfastly maintain observation of negative circumstances. This can be counterproductive because it only sees the difficulties in a situation, which in turn results in more worry and dread. In that case new self-instructions need to be added, such as "scan the perceptual field for potential positive outcomes" and "find ways to reach a positive outcome." These addenda give anxious patients other choices and reduce preoccupation with negative matters.

Yet, a problematic self-instruction with one patient can be useful for another patient. For example, the instruction to "be concerned about potential future problems" is needed for asymptomatic chronic illness patients or noncompliant patients. Neither of these patients takes his/her disease seriously enough. Both need a mild level of anxiety and dread about what could happen in the future if the medical regimen is not followed; instructions to focus on potential problems can do that.

An absolutist policy can cause few problems if supplemented with executive beliefs that avoid emotional and behavioral problems. Again, to reiterate the point of CCT, appropriate executive beliefs can avoid problems created by irrational or unrealistic policy beliefs. Not everyone who thinks irrationally and unrealistically will end up feeling badly or have psychological symptoms. For instance, the policy belief, "Finding a cure is vital," may be unrealistic and cause the individual to become upset when a cure is not found. Yet, with appropriate executive beliefs, that unrealistic policy does not have to be so problematic. Here are examples of helpful executive beliefs:

a. Continue to drive to find a cure, but be self-supportive when disappointed about not finding one.
b. Don't be hypercritical or lambaste the body or health care providers when a cure is not found.
c. Remain optimistic. Don't become negative.

5. *Dysfunction is not usually a matter of ineptitude or inadequacy but a lack of knowledge, experience, time, and a failure to learn from past mistakes.*

Many strategies can be beneficial but are abandoned because patients do not take the time and trouble to develop the skills that can turn a strategy into a success. For example, a medical patient who knows that she must be assertive with family members to gain their help may stop asserting herself when her efforts do not meet immediate success. She needs a support skill like persistence, but that motivational ability takes time and work to develop. Neglecting to develop it impedes the development of assertiveness and limits success. When that happens the patient may wrongly abandon assertiveness because "it's not working."

In summary, coping skills therapy follows a training paradigm, where something must be done over and over before proficiency is achieved. So often patients will think of themselves as simply inept or inadequate when they cannot attain a goal, when the real culprit is insufficient time spent on developing a coping response. Time and experience are needed to develop a fluid performance of a skill. Providers need to educate patients about the vital importance of practice, practice, and more practice.

Another reason patients do not attain goals is because providers do not adequately teach them how to perform a skill. Providers often give a useful strategy but fail to teach the skills that will make the strategy succeed. In a coping skills model, a provider must be an adequate teacher and carefully explain how a skill will operate, where it can be used, and when to use it.

Furthermore, providers have to adequately induct a patient into using a skill to increase motivation to practice it. Providers have to know what will make a strategy succeed. This means knowing the links in a coping skills chain. If the provider leaves out an important link in the chain, then a patient may flounder and think of herself as inept. A past mistake should inform both the provider and patient that another link in the chain is required. Instead of abandoning a strategy when it is ineffective, providers need to reassess what skills are needed to make it work.

Past situations in general are a great teacher. Patients need to dissect a successful situation to discover what skills were utilized in that context and then continue to use them in the future to ensure success. Conversely, patients need to assess unsuccessful, problematic situations to assess if a skill was used excessively or should not have been used at all in that context. This way of operating parallels the solutions-oriented model that follows this same practice (de Shazer, 1985, 1988, 1991).

Summary

People will naturally compose strategies to accomplish a goal, and then set skills to fulfill the strategy. Any skill has benefit if used in the proper amount, context, time, and with other appropriate skills. Problems can also arise if a skill is lacking. The skills play out the strategy and policy belief.

Chapter 3

Phases in Adaptation

D isease is handed to people. It is an affecting force and a given that must be addressed. One way or another, people have to respond to that force in their lives by making adjustments. What needs to be addressed in the disease process and how people adjust to it is the subject of this chapter.

While diseases and their respective symptoms differ, the experience of chronic illness is similar. Likewise, the experience of terminal illness has significant similarities across diseases. Moreover, both chronic and terminal illness patients must deal with many of the same challenges and problems. Both groups have to contend with the same emotions and issues stimulated by the disease experience: anger, guilt, anxiety, bitterness, deprivation, uncertainty, rejection, frustration, discomfort, suffering, and helplessness.

Both chronic and terminal illness patients move through the same phases regarding common needs and goals. However, patients may not necessarily move through those phases in a linear fashion. Some get stuck in a particular phase and make little progress. Some move forward and backward in a pendulous fashion. Some make a quick adjustment and have good adaptation but regress when their medical situation takes a sudden turn for the worse. And some who have the appropriate coping skills meet the tasks and resolve the challenges of each phase. They learn to adjust to their disease so it does not dominate their life. The needed skills for each phase are listed for moving on to a higher level of functioning.

In this chapter we will discuss five phases in the treatment of chronic and terminal illness: a) crises phase, b) postcrisis phase, c) alienation phase, d) consolidation phase, and e) synthesis phase. Some of these phases have tasks that must be resolved in order to progress. See manual and disc for questionnaire to assess patient's phase of adjustment.

CRISIS PHASE

When disease first enters a person's life, it usually creates a feeling of crisis. There is shock and alarm along with abhorrence and nonacceptance of what is happening. Insecurity is acute because the person feels threatened. Instability and disorder mark the crisis phase. Changes in body functioning cause changes in everyday life. What previously organized life no longer does. The habits and roles that structured existence are precluded or interfered with by symptoms of the disease or its treatment. The routines that gave life regularity come to a sudden stop or proceed inconsistently (Fennell, 2001).

There is also instability in identity and self-image. Negative self-representations develop as symptoms progress; the more symptoms affect functioning, the worse the person thinks of him/herself. Inevitably, an unwanted persona is forced on patients that alter previous self-images.

Life becomes chaotic. There is a lack of cohesion between goals. On one hand there is a push to maintain a former way of life, and on the other hand there is a need to adjust to the current situation. This is revealed in a lack of direction and uncertainty about what to do next. The ability to predict and make basic commitments about time and allocation of energy becomes limited. Small changes in symptoms seem crucial. There is a preoccupation with symptoms that are scrutinized for meaning. Any sign of further ill health or infirmity becomes a portent of future demise. Many patients experience an oscillation between disability and full functioning that leaves them confused and uncertain. On some days change is moving toward improvement and on other days toward deterioration. While life appears to be at a turning point, in actuality turning points become weekly occurrences. Critical moments in body functioning or appearance become commonplace.

Symptomatic patients are forced to face the reality that everything they care about may be crumbling before their very eyes, but they are unable to stop it. What gave patients meaning in the past seems to be slipping through their grasp. A pervasive fear suffuses daily activities; worry becomes a pastime. Reality appears harsh, cruel, and punitive. The body seems unreliable and untrustworthy, causing patients to be perplexed and unsure of what this new, unsound body can produce, for them, their loved ones, or their employer. Not feeling, acting, or looking like their old selves, feeling invaded and besieged by hostile forces that have seized hold of their bodies, the medical patient lives in fear of "Who will I become?"

PRECIPITANTS

The sense of crisis can be precipitated by one of several developments. Most commonly it is brought on by symptom onset. A slow progression of symptoms keeps reminding patients that a condition is brewing that cannot be ignored. A sudden, dramatic appearance of symptoms feels overwhelming and takes the patient aback; instability, in a heartbeat, replaces a well-balanced world.

Yet, in some patients, symptoms do not precipitate a crisis. They stay calm and do not jump to conclusions about the future. They wait to see what treatment can offer them. Filled with hope that medication, surgery, prayer, or time will lead to a cure, they continue to lead normal lives with minimal apprehension. Faith in higher powers such as doctors, God, or drug companies buoys the spirits. Crisis only ensues when that higher power seems unable to deliver salvation, or when time fails to heal.

There are other patients who bear their symptoms admirably and have no crisis, providing their old lifestyle is not disturbed. They can march on through thick and thin, as long as role maintenance is not threatened. The feeling of crisis begins only when symptoms overcome role functioning and patterned existence. At that point, the realization looms that disease is insidious, and that they will not be able to dodge the bullet heading directly toward them.

Other patients enter the crisis phase when they receive a diagnosis of chronic or terminal disease. Until that time they may have ignored their symptoms or treated their condition in a blasé, perfunctory manner. They had hope that their condition can be remedied. As long as the assortment of random symptoms had no name, they were able to cope. Assigning a name to an assemblage of symptoms suddenly changed the meaning of the situation. Patients then have to realize what the word "chronic" or "terminal" really means, that their disease may stay with them or kill them, but it will not go away. The sad facts have to be confronted that an unwanted condition causing physical and psychological suffering will change their life in varying degrees. Just knowing that, the level of psychological suffering increases and often are several fold.

There are other patients who only enter the crisis phase when suffering becomes too much to bear. They may know that they have a chronic or terminal condition but ignore it as long as their level of suffering is manageable. When suffering becomes intolerable their stable life feels shaky. They are unable to cope any longer and begin to hate their suffering and seek an end to it, which will not be found.

The course for asymptomatic patients is uneven. Some drift in and out of crisis. While seemingly healthy, they know they have a condition that can become symptomatic and profoundly alter their very existence. The sword of Damocles hangs over their heads, and when they realize that, some slip into crisis. Other asymptomatic patients live their lives as if nothing had gone wrong. They have no crisis phase until symptoms surface or the doctor or significant others issue stern warnings that a change in habits or behavior is mandatory. Once they face the need for a required lifestyle change their crisis phase begins, but it can also evaporate in denial.

Finally, crisis can recur when a personal caretaker ceases to function as a caretaker (Pittman, 1987). For instance, the patient's doctor leaves the medical practice, a spouse seeks marital separation, or a child leaves for college. The caretaker maintained order in the patient's life and with his/her absence disorder is ignited.

DREAM CRUSH

When patients finally enter the crisis phase, they face a state that this book calls "*dream crush.*" This is a condition where the fondest hopes for the future that usually have been in place for many years disintegrate. The road to the Promised Land must either take a wide detour or may be closed permanently. If the patient believes the former, then s/he will be highly frustrated but the crisis phase can be mitigated to some extent. But if patients believe the latter, then the feeling of crisis over-shadows everything else.

A major cause of dream crush is *self-placement.* This is where people place themselves where they think they should be at a certain age in their life. Self-placement seeks a particular, specified existence with a set lifestyle, socioeconomic status, and financial condition. It establishes what type of life is expected, if not demanded. It details how the body, mind, or appearance should be.

As long as there are means to reach that self-placement, life remains steady. People feel good about themselves for accomplishing long-term goals. However, the advent of disease can sharply hinder or terminate the dream. When self-placement is foiled or strongly compromised, people experience it as a narcissistic insult. The good feeling about themselves takes a blow. They feel inadequate and incapable of attaining valued goals. When that happens, disenchantment with self ensues; dejection sharply rises.

Sometimes, dream crush is a reality. In the case of some disabling and terminal diseases, life will end and along with that comes foreclosure on the dream. Other times, though, dream crush is only imagined or partly true. In either case, even with loss of parts or all of the dream, happiness can still be maintained by other venues as long as patients are flexible and willing to take a different road to the Promised Land.

TASKS OF THE CRISIS PHASE

There are two general tasks for medical patients. One task is knowing how to deal with crisis in general. While the state of crisis usually follows the initial outbreak of symptoms or when the diagnosis is first received, it can recur many times over the course of the disease. It can happen when the condition worsens months or years later, when the medical situation is no longer stable, or when the patient leaves remission. Hence, learning crisis management skills is of prime importance to medical patients. Part II discusses four general coping skills that will reduce the feeling of crisis whenever it occurs.

A second general task is acquiring self-efficacy. Medical patients feel in crisis when they lack self-efficacy. A lack of self-efficacy is the belief that the individual is unable to influence the outcome of the situation (Bandura, 1977, 1997). For medical patients, there is a belief that they are unable to manage their symptoms along with the consequences of having those symptoms. However, the feeling of crisis will decrease when medical patients believe that they know what to do to manage their situation. Self-assurance promises that there is competency and that will avoid a feeling of crisis. Overall, the skills discussed here will help build a feeling of self-efficacy, so disease will not appear to be overwhelming.

There are *four specific tasks* facing medical patients in crisis.

1) They need a policy on how to address their suffering and what to do when suffering is felt. The fact is, medical patients will not be able to avoid suffering. Disease and the treatment for it will cause suffering in varying degrees.

2) They need to know how to manage physical discomfort. When these two tasks are achieved, having a disease and being treated for it will not appear so daunting or onerous.

3)   This task involves coping with changes in identity. Loss of role functioning would not feel as bad as it does if patients did not have an identity that demanded it. Conversely, disease would not be so frustrating if patients' identity allowed for role decrement and inability to meet role duties. Crisis occurs because identity is being battered and challenged, standards for self are unyielding, and expectations will not be reasonable. Hence, a crucial task is preserving identity as much as possible while forming a new identity that allows for the changes brought by disease.

4)   Finally, the effects of disease are devastating and require substantial emotional support. Medical patients need assurance that they can gain this support when needed. Securing support from others is quite helpful but often that is not enough nor forthcoming when patients ask for it. Taking this into consideration, a final task of the crisis phase is building a self-support capacity. This involves developing a helpful, nurturing way of relating to oneself.

To accomplish these tasks, four specific skills are needed and if present can lead the patient into a postcrisis phase. Part II discusses those skills. First, there is the skill of assimilation of suffering. It is in part a philosophy and in part a method to manage suffering. The tactics for performing that skill will be discussed in Chapter 4. Second, there is the skill for ameliorating physical discomfort and coping with frustration about bodily symptoms. Those skills are presented in Chapter 5. Third, there are skills for preserving a positive identity as well as maintaining the old identity, and they are discussed in Chapter 6. Finally, self-support skills are listed in Chapter 7.

Together, these four skills will help stabilize the medical situation and ease the sense of crisis. They will provide crisis management ability and develop self-efficacy to avoid future crises. Once someone knows how to cope in a crisis situation, s/he will not be as reluctant to move into the future to face what will happen next. Turning points will not feel as scary when patients are able to say with confidence, "I can handle this situation." In summary, a skills orientation creates self-efficacy which in turn obviates the medical crisis.

POSTCRISIS PHASE

Following the resolution of crisis, patients enter a postcrisis phase with two main features. One feature is stabilization. Once deterioration reaches a plateau and the disease stops progressing, patients are able to return to work and resume most of their duties at home. Anomie, at this point, ends with the resurrection of role duties. Life feels regular when old patterns and habits are resumed. Life seems more orderly. Self-representations that once comforted and bolstered self-esteem (e.g., being an able worker or mom) are reexperienced.

Terminal illness patients in the postcrisis phase have had time to get over some of the shock that they will eventually die. They have had time to get their estate in order, to ready their family for life without them, and to begin to sort through the many emotions they now experience. Likewise, disabled patients have had time to become familiar with changes in role functioning and their new lifestyle. They are finding ways to meet their needs. The life of a disabled person is no longer so shocking. This does not mean that chronic or terminal illness patients are not disturbed by what has happened to their lives, or that they have resolved any of their emotional issues.

A second feature of the postcrisis phase is the absence of crisis. The tumult and upheaval in the patient's life has subsided; the internal state no longer feels disheveled. Patients feel relief and are not as fearful. Life no longer seems so precarious or at a turning point. Now more familiar with their symptoms and treatment side effects, they have become accustomed to following the medical regimen. In general, they feel "things have calmed down."

If we would use the word "stabilization" to characterize this period, though, it would give a false picture because that term is essentially positive in nature. The postcrisis phase can be positive but also may be quite negative, if it merges into an alienation phase (see below). Further, the stability of the postcrisis phase does not rest on a solid foundation. Many forces such as a resurgence of symptoms, loss of a job, or an absent caretaker can cause immediate decompensation. Many patients move back and forth between crisis and postcrisis, depending on the current state of their body. That occurs when they lack the coping skills discussed in Part II, so any deterioration can result in crisis.

Yet, if patients can meet certain tasks and acquire vital skills, then they can progress to a higher level of functioning—the consolidation phase. They can move from postcrisis to consolidation and make a solid adjustment to disease. Or, they can proceed into alienation where negative emotions dominate. Hence, *the postcrisis period is a crossroads* for medical patients, and providers need to make them realize how crucial this period is.

ALIENATION PHASE

The fright that was felt when symptoms first arose is replaced by the knowledge that those same symptoms will limit or block need fulfillment. Reality at this time becomes intrusive and cannot be dodged by denial or discounting of the facts. It makes a scarring impression that the body will never be the same as it once was.

A common response to this realization is alienation from the body. A patient dissociates from his/her body and views it from the outside as an object. The core self, with its intellect, spirit, and emotions, becomes psychologically distant from the body. Whatever caring existed toward the body is withdrawn as part of the disaffection process, typified by either hostility or indifference. Hostility toward the body can be expressed as rejection and dislike of it, or unwillingness to be accommodating to the body's limited capacity.

In part, alienation from the body is an emotional reaction to how the body has changed for the worse. In another regard it is a coping strategy to avoid diminishing self-esteem. The "bad" parts of the person—the corporal self—is separated from the "good" or core self. Once this is accomplished, a patient can vent anger at his/her body with impunity because it is no longer part of the self. Alienation also allows a patient to make life into an object. Once psychologically distant from it, negative emotions such as bitterness can be directed at it for causing so much suffering for the patient and his/her loved ones.

The alienation from self is due to an inability to meet expectations and standards of role duties. The self is put down instead of being supported. Conversely, there can be alienation from those roles when they become oppressive and a burden. Because of symptoms or treatment side effects, roles become harder to maintain. Trying to maintain them becomes costly, toilsome, and enervating. To avoid self-criticism about not fulfilling role duties, patients can devalue roles that they once cherished.

Adding to the estrangement that the patient feels, others can also become estranged from the patient. Spouses, children, other family members, friends, or employers who were once supportive when symptoms first arose, after a while grow less patient and friendly and more demanding as the disease continues. They respond to the patient with less love, caring, and respect. A vicious circle ensues. Their estrangement from the patient, usually expressed as indifference, impatience, hostility, or outright severing of the relationship, causes the patient to feel alienated from them. This isolation and loss of support occurs when patients need support most!

The alienation phase can last for weeks, months, or even years. If chronic illness patients utilize a maladaptive coping strategy or do not learn how to cope with their emotions, they may remain stuck in this phase indefinitely. In the case of terminal illness, patients can die feeling alienated, leaving the world bitter, rejecting their body, and angry at life or God for what has happened to them. (Not all medical patients go through an alienation phase. It is much more common with symptomatic than asymptomatic disease, because the latter results in far fewer changes in the patient's life.)

When discussing alienation with patients, providers should discuss it quantitatively as occurring on a continuum from high to low. After defining it, ask patients how much they feel that way. To resolve alienation, there are tasks patients must deal with.

TASKS OF THE ALIENATION PHASE

Inevitably most medical patients will feel some degree of bitterness that arises from having a life disrupted or sidetracked. That bitterness will need to be disposed of or else it will poison the spirit and harm relationships with others. Hence, one major task is finding ways to neutralize that bitterness.

Disease will cause alterations in the body, how it functions, or how it appears. The body may not be able to perform as it did previously. To live within one's body, a medical patient will need to forge a rapprochement with his corporal self. S/he will need to know how to accommodate the body. If the patient considers his or her body disfigured, then the task is to alter the negative formulation of self in order to avoid a loss of self-esteem and a feeling of inferiority.

Inevitably there will be some degree of uncertainty caused by symptoms. Patients must learn how to manage uncertainty and reduce it. They will need to know how to deal with the future that appears so frightening.

Three skills are presented to help patients overcome alienation. One is uncertainty tolerance (discussed in Chapter 8) to reduce anxiety while providing ways to make uncertainty less of a problem. A second skill is bitterness disposal (discussed in Chapter 9). Two support skills for avoiding bitterness are presented: rejection tolerance and disappointment accommodation. A third skill is body accommodation (discussed in Chapter 10). A protocol is offered for how to relate to the body differently. In addition, tactics are given for treating disfigurement. With the help of these skills, patients can feel more unified and less antagonistic toward themselves and others. This will help them acquire a feeling of consolidation.

CONSOLIDATION PHASE

The consolidation phase is a time where patients no longer feel as if their lives are coming apart at the seams. Rather oppositely, the medical patient feels solidified and stronger, as if "things are coming together now for me." In this phase they feel more in control of their life and far less helpless than they did in the crisis phase. They believe that they can rely on their body more and more, even if that body is incapacitated or not functioning any differently than when symptoms first arose. They believe that they can meet more of their own needs, even though they are less able. They trust that their bodies can still satisfy them, even if they cannot function as they did in the premorbid state. Whatever alienation from the body existed has eased substantially. In total, the patient feels far more secure although still possessing an infirm body.

While hardly liking bodily symptoms or appearing different, patients in this phase no longer feel outraged about being that way. Having symptoms does not disturb them nearly as much as it used to, even though they continue to wish that their symptoms never existed. While they regret being symptomatic, they are not filled with regret about what has happened to their lives. While they suffer from these symptoms, there is greater acceptance of being symptomatic. While they find having symptoms as foul, they are no longer at war with their bodies or look at them as the enemy. They no longer feel distant from their body nor reject it; the mind-body split has been healed to a greater extent. While they do not like nor want their chronic or terminal disease, they have stopped hating it. They may say that they hate their disease and its symptoms, but the word "hate" is used mostly in an intellectual way, as an evaluation of their condition. They are not beset by the passion of hatred.

The feeling of consolidation is shown in other ways. Patients in this phase can offer themselves support and compassion, which makes themselves feel stronger and more set in their lives. The needs of the medical patient can be incorporated into daily life without shame or deep regret. Those who were involved in religion but felt alienated from God for not answering prayers for a cure, begin to return to church or synagogue.

In this phase, there is also a consolidation of the patient with other people. After enduring alienation from other people, some of those relationships have been healed, or the patient has stopped feeling so distraught about significant other's behavior. There is more acceptance of the negative treatment of others, because patients better understand their limitations and why others acted as they did. This does not mean there is approval of others' conduct or surrender to misconduct. Patients have had time to convert significant others into more appropriate sources of support. If relationships have ended, patients have had time to find new ones that can offer more support. Often this is with people who have the same condition or even another disease. If a patient is still working, the employer and coworkers have had time to adjust their expectations of the patient. There is a better working relationship between employer and patient, patient and coworkers.

There is also a coming together of self-representations. Patients have combined the pre-illness identity with the identity developed after symptom onset (e.g., "I am a mother and I am physically weak"). Images of the old and new can be blended together without nearly as much antagonism or distaste. Most importantly, they are able to coexist with their new identity, even though it was not anticipated.

In summary, while medical patients may evaluate the quality of their life as bad and disapprove of how their lives have developed, they do allow those changes into their life. They no longer actively protest their disease or damn life or fortune for causing them sorrow. There is greater willingness to coexist with what they do not want, assimilate suffering into their life, tolerate frustration, and accommodate to being a chronic or terminal illness patient.

To highlight the differences between the alienation and consolidation phases, let's compare two patients. Alfred is 70 years old and loves life. He deeply resents having to die because he maintains that he has lots more life to live. He fights against the idea of dying and is quite depressed about his terminal illness. He cannot accept that his life will be ending in the next few months and feels bitter about that. He damns God for cutting short his retirement and hates his body for being weak and hurting.

Brian, on the other hand, is 20 years old and has been battling his terminal illness for several years. He, too, wants to be like his peers and live an exciting, fun-filled existence. He, too, hates his disease, but more on an intellectual level. But unlike Alfred, he has accepted it into his life and is no longer at war with the idea of dying. He is not at war with his body and even finds good things that it can offer him in his limited capacity. While he feels sad when he thinks about dying or not being like others, he is resigned to his fate and able to submit to forces greater than himself.

Tasks of the Consolidation Phase

While there are many positive gains in the consolidation phase, there is still more work to be done. The disease or treatment has changed the patient and his functioning in several regards. Old patterns that previously offered meaning have been terminated or abridged. Old goals have been put on hold or permanently halted because they cannot be attained now. This leads to two problems.

One problem is a loss of meaning. New directions, goals, and behaviors will have to be developed that take into consideration the changes in the body due to the disease or treatment. At the same time there are many interests and values that still persist from the premorbid state, but they cannot be pursued as vigorously as they once were. Yet, patients seek to resume them in a limited way. Consequently, there is a need to integrate facets of the old and new life.

A second problem is coming to terms with limitations, accepting what cannot be done any longer. Also, while working to improve their relationships with others, medical patients must also deal with the limitations of others. Overall, coming to terms with limitations allows patients to make peace with how their life has changed.

Two skills will be used to achieve these two goals. One skill is meaning-making, discussed in Chapter 11. The second skill, discussed in Chapter 12, is limitation management, a two-part skill that involves deprivation allowance and helplessness tolerance. As a consequence of these two skills working together, patients can move onto a higher level of functioning—the synthesis phase.

SYNTHESIS PHASE

Synthesizing involves unifying the individual. There is the unifying of values and goals of the healthy person with the sick person. For instance, the sick person may want to rest and the healthy person may want activity. Bringing opposing goals together without regret or remorse is a function of synthesis.

There is the unifying of varying states of the body. On some days the patient may feel healthy and not encumbered by disease, while on other days the disease may weigh heavily on him/her. Medical patients can almost feel as if they were two people. Synthesis allows the patient to feel at ease switching from the healthy to the sick. Both become parts of self. The sick part is not hated when it appears, because synthesis decreases consternation about switching from feeling good to bad.

Synthesis also involves combining limitation with interest. Someone may desire to do something but has to take into consideration what can be realistically accomplished. Synthesizing involves a constant blending of need, medical requirements, body incapacity, needs of the medical regimen, and spousal and family needs.

There is the synthesis of old and new interests to form a more cohesive way of satisfying needs. For example, Jill, an MS patient, loved to pursue outdoor activities before she became disabled. She would take long walks and bicycle avidly. This became impossible once she developed MS. However, she synthesized her old interest with reality concerns and came up with a new pursuit: she reads in a natural setting like a park and takes short, abbreviated walks of only a few minutes duration that do not tire her.

The synthesis of identities from the crisis phase continues to be pursued. Ways are found to express the essence of self as a medical patient. For instance, Jack was a physically fit person who exercised regularly before he became a paraplegic. He continued to lift weights in his wheel chair. Linda loved to dance before she became physically incapacitated. While no longer able to dance, she learned Tai Chi to continue to express her interest in grace and form.

A major synthesis is becoming a whole person despite being a medical patient, someone who feels normal, like everyone else in many ways, except for the fact that s/he has a disease. The disease and the person have now become one. The disease has become part of the person, but just one facet of the self, and no longer dominating the perception of self.

Summary

The first phase medical patients enter is a crisis time, which generally occurs at symptom onset or when the diagnosis is given. Dream crush is a major reason for crisis. This is followed by a postcrisis time when patients become more stable. Two options can occur at this point: a movement into alienation where bodily changes are rejected or a consolidation time when the person feels closer to his/her body. This requires resolution of bitterness, management of uncertainty, and accommodation to bodily changes. Accomplishing this can lead patients to a new lifestyle where they find new sources of meaning as they come to terms with limitations. At each phase there are tasks and skills that need to be learned in order to resolve those tasks and move on to a higher state of adjustment.

Part II

Coping Skills for Crisis Phase

Chapter 4

Assimilation of Suffering

P atients frequently disallow their disease and refuse to accept its existence. One key facet of the disease experience that is not allowed is suffering. Yet, suffering quickly becomes one of the salient issues medical patients have to address, as their lives are soon taken over by it. Health care providers need to closely watch how patients respond to suffering, to assess if their response helps or hinders adaptation. This chapter will discuss an irrational, maladaptive response to suffering and then offers a rational, adaptive substitute that is termed the *assimilation of suffering*.

THE NATURE OF SUFFERING

Suffering is the feeling of distress and pain, both psychological and/ or physical. The archaic definition of disease aptly distills the experience of suffering: a lack of ease in one's life—dis–ease. It is a state of misery, but it is also a response to misery. It is how the patient *chooses* to act—on a conscious or unconscious level—when faced with a disagreeable, unpleasant, unwanted, distressful activating event.

What are those activating events? What are experiences that commonly result in suffering?

a. Disease of the anatomy results in negative physical sensations such as pain, itching, tingling, burning, bloating, etc. Suffering is both the physical response (e.g., throbbing, burning, aching) and the affective response (e.g., hate, irritation) to anatomical damage. In addition, there is a third component: the evaluation of the physical sensations ("This stinks," "This is not right"). The affective state and the evaluation together comprise the psychological distress that the patient feels from having to endure physical discomfort. This definition of physical suffering is based on Melzack and Wall's gate control model for pain (1970).

b.   Undesirable physical conditions such as muscle weakness, fatigue, tremor, or instability when walking results in distress and frustration. Again, suffering includes the affective response (e.g., fear, frustration) and the evaluation of the physical condition (e.g., "This fatigue is terrible.").

c.   The treatment for the disease and side effects from treatment can result in suffering. Treatment can be painful, onerous, debilitating, or cause loss (e.g., appearance decrements). There is substantial waiting time to see health providers and therapists, and treatment itself can involve substantial time commitments. That in turn causes other problems, such as loss of work or time away from the family. Health providers themselves can also cause suffering by being insensitive or difficult. There are repeated surgeries that cause the patient recurring pain and time away from work during recovery. There is disease that results in surgery that cuts away a part of the body that supports identity, such as the breasts or testicles.

d.   The ongoing uncertainty, worry, and anguish that accompany many diseases frequently result in suffering.

e.   There are difficult, harmful consequences from disease that cause suffering, such as financial loss, job loss, role performance decrement, inability to meet other people's expectations, or adverse, pejorative changes in friendships and family relationships. Again, there is the affective response to those consequences and the evaluative response ("It's awful not being able to work.") to those consequences.

f.   There is suffering due to the loss of a lifestyle or "normal living."

g.   There is suffering stemming from the entire medical experience, such as anger, helplessness, and powerlessness dealing with forces more powerful than the individual (e.g., HMOs, insurance companies, hospitals).

In fact, medical patients can suffer from two diseases. One is the actual disease of the body with its inherent symptoms. In addition, there can be a psychological affliction from not being able to suffer well, from not being able to cope with high levels of pain, distress, loss, and misery. This is the difficulty of not being able to manage the many changes and losses that come with disease. The *inability to suffer is possibly the major cause of depression and suicidal ideation among chronic and terminal illness patients, and not the disease itself.* See manual and disc to assess patient's degree of suffering.

THE REJECTION OF SUFFERING

To sum up, chronic and terminal diseases will result in some degree of suffering that is unavoidable. To state an obvious point, suffering is unpleasant and unwanted. At some point, virtually all chronic and terminal illness patients institute a coping strategy that rejects further suffering. While not wise, adaptive, or rational, the rejection of suffering is a way to address the shocking, jarring realization that the disease and its consequences are permanent for as long as the patient is alive.

While the rejection of suffering is an irrational, maladaptive coping strategy, it does offer some measure of satisfaction by responding to the powerlessness imposed by disease.

- It channels all of the emotions that result from having a disease and having to treat it (e.g., sadness, anger, and anxiety) into a uniform protest ("This is awful—what is happening to me!"). This protest takes a stand against unpleasant sensations, losses, and unremitting, unwanted conditions.
- It facilitates movement through treatment and eases side effects by complaining.
- It provides for venting and catharsis, which reduces frustration.
- It places limits on provider's behavior, bodily sensations, or treatments that cause misery ("No more hurting; I've had it").
- It offers comfort to patients via self-pity ("Why me? I don't deserve this").
- It removes patients from the situation via depression so they do not have to feel further suffering. Depression provides disengagement on both a physical and psychological level.
- It offers patients a final out from their torment—suicide.

The rejection of suffering can be detected in various ways:

- As complaints about the disease. The physical condition is renounced and spoken about derisively.
- As general irritability, impatience, and frequent rages.
- As brooding, dejection, and discontent that is part of depression.
- As difficult, demanding, or cantankerous behavior (e.g., frequent complaining and bickering with others).
- As self-pity, manifested as bemoaning existence.
- As frequent blaming of everything on the disease.
- As hatred of the condition.
- As talk about the limits of one's tolerance ("I cannot go on this way any longer").

- As assertions about fairness ("It's not right what has happened to me").
- Through choice of language, e.g., discussing a cure as imperative.
- Through plaintive or wistful yearnings for the pre-illness "good ol' days."
- Outright, overt rejection of suffering.
- Repudiation or dismissal of family members or health providers who try to help the patient accept the disease.
- Doggedly pursuing a cure in the hope that it can eradicate further suffering.
- As doctor-shopping and treatment-experimentation, again to find the illusive salvation.
- Avoidance of anything that can increase suffering, e.g., seeking a sedentary lifestyle in order to decrease pain and suffering. Decisions about how to live are geared around not aggravating the condition.

While on the surface the goal of eliminating suffering appears to make sense, it is nevertheless maladaptive because it underemphasizes coping with the disease and adjustment. It does not point the patient in the needed direction of learning how to manage and tolerate. The coping strategy is also irrational because it wants an end to something that will not end. By definition, chronic means an unending condition; hence, no cure. Terminal means there will be an eventual end. Even when the disease recedes, enters remission, or becomes asymptomatic, it continues to be a major factor in planning and living life. The fact is that chronic and terminal illness patients will have to face significant suffering that simply comes with the territory. *Rejection of suffering fights against accepting reality and instead seeks to change it.*

Overall, a rejection of suffering strategy causes more problems in the long run. It is actually magical thinking seeking salvation, born out of frustration, futility, and impotency. When patients finally realize that they cannot escape from their situation, suffering, bitterness, hopelessness, and desperation engulf them. When they realize that a cure is not forthcoming, they feel even more desperate and discouraged.

While suffering is not wanted, it does have to be addressed as an unfortunate, unwanted part of life. A way has to be found to coexist and make peace with it. It is the elephant sitting in the living room who will not go away. Ignoring, avoiding, or protesting will not eradicate it. The only way out is assimilation of suffering.

THE ASSIMILATION OF SUFFERING

When suffering occurs, a response tendency—*the assimilation of suffering*—is needed. It is incorporated into activities of daily living as a *response substitution strategy* for the rejection of suffering. Inserted into the cognitive and affective process at prescribed times and places, it interrupts pejorative responses and leads to an alternative stimulus-response chain. The cycle goes as follows: pain escalates, health providers frustrate, treatment drags on, fatigue does not cease, or altered appearance does not change. In each case suffering is felt. Now the patient refuses to suffer any longer. In place of that response, the assimilation of suffering tactic is utilized to override it.

This coping strategy offers several benefits. It reifies abstract ideas like acceptance, forbearance, and forgiveness, so they are able to take on a concrete existence. It allows patients to **allow, accept, and absorb** further distress and discomfort. It halts the protest against suffering. It admits and makes room for negative experiences that cannot be avoided. It makes peace with symptomatology and treatment side effects and facilitates coexistence with them. It allows suffering to be part of everyday movements and activities, so they can recede into the background of the mind. Let's now see how it is presented to patients.

INDUCTION PHASE

To lower resistance to and increase usage of this coping strategy, providers need to present it in the following way. Chronic and terminally ill patients will often rebel against this strategy because it calls for living with suffering, which is the opposite of what they want to hear from health care providers.

First, secure a phenomenological description of the person's experience. What is the disease and the treatment for that patient? Once patients have had ample time to ventilate and express anguish about having a chronic or terminal illness, introduce the idea of assimilating suffering.

You really face an awful situation. You did not want this disease to happen, but it has. That's rotten. It should not be this way, but it is. I can see why you think it is unfair. Disease is not pleasant, and there is a natural urge to reject it. You hate to accept the fact that you are stuck with a condition that will cause you to suffer (or end your life). That's a hard realization to take in. I would think that would make you feel both angry and sad. Anyone would feel that way. It is hard to come to terms with the fact that your life will change (or end) so much now. That, too, is a hard fact to accept. You need to find a way to lower your level of suffering, and I know that is what you want. I have a way for you to do that. Hearing what I have to say, you may think that my strategy is contradictory to what you want. But if you try it out, it can help you in the long run.

Notice that the induction both agrees with and validates the patient's subjective reality, such as rating the disease as awful or rotten. It does not argue with the patient if the subjective reality is correct, as in REBT (Ellis and Abrams, 1994). Changing patients' evaluation of their disease (e.g., "It's awful") is not needed, providing they embrace coping as their primary objective. The induction informs the patient about what reality is, however. CCT does emphasize what is objective reality. Finally, the induction unites the therapist and patient to seek what the latter yearns for—a reduction in suffering. Paradoxically, that will come with assimilation of suffering.

EDUCATION PHASE

Once patients are willing to learn about assimilation of suffering, they can proceed to an education phase where they will learn how the skill can help.

You have a disease that causes you to suffer. That's a terrible thing to have happened to you. But if you know how to suffer, then suffering will not hurt you so much. If you are able to suffer well, you will not be so distressed about having a chronic (or terminal) illness. You may have substantial pain, but the pain will not bother you as much, once you learn the skill I will show you. People may frustrate and disappoint you. You may not be able to complete all of your responsibilities. Your symptoms may continue. All of that will cause you to suffer. But if you know how to suffer well, then the trouble that comes with having a chronic (or terminal) illness will not get to you nearly as much. Knowing how to cope can lessen the amount of suffering you feel overall.

Once patients are interested in learning how the skill operates, the therapist presents the three subskills that comprise this ability.

Acceptance

Acceptance is a mind-set and internal activity. It is commonly confused with surrender. The former is a mind-set for a situation, while the latter is a behavior. The behavior involves two options: surrender (suspend behavior trying to change a situation), or not surrender (seek a way to change the situation). With acceptance comes an affective state of grace, a peace of mind, and tranquility. Main ideas of acceptance:

- Realization that suffering—distress, discomfort—is an unavoidable by-product of chronic or terminal illness. The focus is on understanding and recognizing what is objective reality.
- Allowance of the fact that suffering and disease will exist because neither can be eradicated. Effort is expended on not hating this fact nor rejecting disease.
- Disallowance of hatred of reality. That keeps the unpleasant fact that disease will be a part of life in the foreground of the mind.
- Acceptance of the fact that a cure will not be forthcoming—at least for now. A cure may be found in the future, but if suffering is occurring in the present, then no cure is available now. Willingness is present to live with the inability to alter disease processes that are essentially beyond the self.
- Recognition that diseases are not supposed to be pleasant. Symptoms show a breakdown in normal anatomical functioning and are supposed to remove ease from a person's life. They inform the person that something is wrong. Patients are urged to face up to this fact with all of its implications.
- Acceptance of the necessity that coping with symptoms and suffering are most important and need to be of the highest priority.

While this message is grim, there is an underlying premise that embracing reality will make people feel better in the long run. Essentially, the assimilation of suffering forces medical patients to confront the disease's harsh, dark reality head on: "This is your lot in life. It is a heavy load to bear, but it is your load and only you can carry it." Because the message is grim, it must be delivered in a caring, inspirational way.

Forbearance

At this point, the second subskill, *forbearance*, is promoted. This is a different way to define suffering—to bear or *suffer one's fate gracefully* as part of the daily passage through life. The patient is asked to show patience, tolerance, and restraint in the face of provocation—provocation from one's body, uncaring, demanding family or coworkers, or health providers showing little compassion. To be able to endure harm, injury, loss, or punishment now becomes the goal. Once such endurance is achieved, the patient can gain a heroic transcendence over unfortunate circumstances that might otherwise result in bitterness and disenchantment with life. Hence, the assimilation of suffering helps people to endure, suffer with dignity, and free themselves from the endless regret of what life should have become.

Forgiveness

The third subskill is *forgiveness*. This includes excusing one's body for coming down with the disease, and God, fate, or fortune for causing it. Forgiveness entails renouncing anger and resentment for having such a hard life to bear. It means overlooking the failings of the body, oneself, or others such as health providers. It means not holding the self accountable for years of smoking, drinking, drugging, and/or poor health habits that may have contributed to the disease. The patient lives with the consequences from his/her actions without rancor, disgust, self-criticism, or self-downing.

There are major benefits from incorporating this coping strategy. It helps patients avoid the vortex of self-pity and the corrosive effects from bitterness over having a painful existence, a lesser life compared with healthy people. This strategy integrates and absorbs suffering into everyday life experience so that it does not remain in the foreground of consciousness. When suffering drifts into the background, the perceived intensity of it is reduced. Misery no longer is the dominant life experience, and that allows other, more positive experiences to reach the foreground. Suffering then becomes a routine *but unwanted* aspect of daily life. When this happens, the secondary disorder from chronic illness—the inability to suffer the body's symptomatology—is ameliorated. Once the patient has been inducted into assimilating his/her suffering, the next step is teaching the tactics for accomplishing it in daily life.

TACTICS

These tactics can be implemented in any of the following situations.

   1)   The patient faces a situation that will increase his/her level of suffering (e.g., cleaning the house, getting out of bed, or completing a

work assignment). Have the patient monitor the activity and evaluate the level of suffering while performing it, from zero to five, with five being extreme suffering. This is a *misery or distress rating.*

2) The patient has a moderate to severe level of suffering (a level of three or higher on the scale from zero to five) at that moment in time.

3) The patient has a moderate to severe level of negative emotion (e.g., anger, frustration, sadness) concerning his disease, symptoms, or treatment side effects on a scale from zero to five.

4) The patient manifests a sign of rejection of suffering.

A. SELF-INSTRUCTION TRAINING

Self-instruction training (Meichenbaum, 1977) is one method of inculcating the beliefs supporting the assimilation of suffering. It will also be used to avoid and counteract the rejection of suffering. The dialogue directs what the patient will think about and how to respond to situations. The self-instructions have several purposes:

- To direct a person to think a desired, rational, realistic thought, e.g., "My symptoms are part of my life now. Accept them?
- To direct the self to engage in self-evaluation, e.g., to check the level of pain or anger about suffering.
- To cue a coping skill, such as relaxation or problem solving.
- To cease an automatic way of responding, such as the maladaptive coping strategy of rejection of suffering (e.g., "Don't fall into hating the disease").
- To initiate and guide the use of a desired behavior (e.g., "Be assertive and tell him I feel too tired to do this").
- To motivate the self, offer encouragement, and inspire desired behavior (e.g., "I can do this even though I am in pain").

The patient and therapist design the dialogue together for all phases of an activity. First the therapist acts as a role model and repeats the self-instructions out loud and then silently. The reason for this is to show the patient that the self-dialogue becomes part of internal speech. The patient says the words out loud and then silently. Situations are then listed where the dialogue is to be used, such as when pain becomes severe. See manual and disc for handouts to patients to develop assimilation of suffering.

The self-dialogue is written for each phase of a situation that could result in suffering: a) before beginning that activity, b) when first experiencing suffering, and c) when feeling most incensed about the abject quality of life. Here is an example of a self-dialogue for a chronic illness patient.*** The dialogue works to inculcate acceptance, forbearance, and forgiveness.

Self-Talk Before Beginning Activities

I am about to start this activity. It will not be easy. I will feel pain and that will be upsetting. Prepare for it.

Let the disease run its course. Let it do its thing. Allow the symptoms to exist. They cannot be avoided.

Don't be afraid of the symptoms. I can handle them.

Don't hate the disease. Don't hate the symptoms. They are a part of me.

My body is me. Don't hate my body. Don't hate what my body has become.

Live with the difficulties while doing tasks. Don't get agitated.

Put my attention to other things. Don't dwell on what's distressing.

It would be preferable if I didn't have this disease but I do have it.

I must accept the disease. Live with it. It's part of me now.

Suffer my disease well. I want to feel proud of myself. I can bear this.

Don't be angry with my body for getting sick. Forgive it.

Self-Talk While Experiencing Suffering

I am going to suffer while doing this normal life activity and that has to be accepted. It comes with having a chronic illness.

Completing this activity is difficult, but I can do it. I can bear up.

Things will not come as easily as they used to. Accept that. Don't get mad because life isn't as easy as it used to be.

I feel some pain. Don't get mad about it.

Don't hate the pain. Pain is just part of my life now, a part of me. Let it in. Don't try to keep it out. It will feel worse if I do.

Don't be at war with my pain.

Don't make my distress foreground. Notice what's pleasant in this situation, regardless of the pain.

Self-Talk When Hatred of Illness Rises

I'm having problems dealing with my illness. I hate being in pain. That means I am fighting reality. That's not good.

Hating this disease means I hate my body. Focus on what I like about my body and not on what I hate about it.

Don't get angry. Take a few deep breaths. Relax.

My suffering cannot be avoided. I can live with it. I'm tough.

I can stand having this condition if I choose to.

I will feel worse when I hate what my body is doing.

I don't want to get involved in thinking that this isn't fair, that I don't deserve this. Thinking that way will only make me feel worse.

B. IMAGERY

Imagery can also be used to assimilate suffering into everyday life. It, too, operates as a response substitution when rejection of suffering occurs. For example:

> Turbulent waters are crashing into a wall with a gate in the middle. The turbulent water stands for rejection and hatred of symptomatology and suffering. Then the gate opens and the water comes rushing in violently, threatening to wash over everything inside the walls. This stands for the initial shock of realizing that suffering will become part of your life, and how much it will negatively dominate life. After a few minutes the waters spread and become calm. The calm water represents you accepting suffering, and being willing to suffer your plight. The water at this point is absorbed onto the land and not noticed any more.

There is also real-time imagery, where a fantasy makes an invisible process visible. For example, the patient visualizes an ice cube that represents pain, diminishing with the aid of medication, heat, or exercise.

C. THERAPEUTIC METAPHORS

Therapeutic metaphors (Haley, 1967; Haley, 1973; Bandler and Grinder, 1975; Gordon, 1978; Gordon and Myers-Anderson, 1981; Zeig, 1980) gives patients a different perspective on the same set of facts. In the example below, the metaphor is given to the conscious mind.

> *Don, an angina patient, felt deeply saddened about the precarious nature of his heart disease that could kill or cripple him at any time. He was suffering from loss of self-esteem and thinking of his body as inadequate, weak, and crumbling. The therapist gave him a metaphor that he could use when he "fell into" this pejorative self-concept.*

> While you can think of yourself in several ways, I want to give you one way to see yourself. You are like a grand old house that has weathered many storms and seasons. While the house does have extensive structural damage in many places, it is still quite capable of providing its occupants with many good years of use. This is a home with history and unique charms. New homes don't have the look of these grand old homes.

Metaphors can also be delivered in an indirect way as part of casual conversation. In that case they are aimed at the unconscious. In this example, the therapist makes small talk with a cancer patient suffering from uncertainty about her future. The therapist nonchalantly brings up what he is thinking of doing that summer—taking his family to see relatives in Colorado. The therapist then reminisces about an experience he had many years ago.

> I was taking this raft trip down a very pretty, rugged river in Utah. The river was breathtaking. We had this experienced guide take us downstream, and that made me feel quite safe, even though the currents were moving very fast. I was not even fazed by how dangerous this experience could be. We were having a relaxing time and everything was wonderful, when all of a sudden we descended down a small waterfall and landed on a rock that could not be seen from the surface. We were suspended and unable to move off the rock. The guide said that this was very dangerous because we could flip over and anything could happen in the swirling water. The trip that started out so safely had suddenly become quite perilous. We were all very worried and I was scared. While we were stuck on that rock, not knowing what would happen next, I started looking around at the river, seeing it from a unique angle. Stuck a few feet below the oncoming water, I was eye level with the swift water coming directly at us, but then it slipped underneath us. Sitting on that rock, in that dangerous position, I had a chance to experience this amazing sight.

The therapist delivers this metaphor without explaining it, that life is a powerful river that is both beautiful and dangerous at the same time. He gives the patient another way to view life, as not just depriving. He wants her to see that even in uncertain, dangerous times there are still wonderful things to behold if someone wants to notice them.

D. SYMBOLIC GESTURING

Symbolic gesturing is a technique that uses a physical movement to create an internal state. It can be combined with self-instructions or imagery. When patients notice that they feel upset and are engaging in rejection of suffering, the symbolic gesture is deployed. For example:

- A slowly moving, horizontal hand gesture stands for a calm life gained by assimilation of suffering. If imagery is combined with this, the patient can imagine a calm, flat ocean along with the hand movement.
- The hands can slowly move toward the body, as if the person is pressing something into him/herself. This stands for letting suffering into the patient's life. If self-instructions are combined with this, the patient can say a small phrase to him/herself like, "Let it be" or "Let it in" as the movement is occurring.
- The hands can slowly push away from the person, as if gaining breathing room from the disease and its symptoms.
- The hands cascade down like a waterfall, to stand for water running off a duck's back. The water is other people's criticism of the patient for not meeting their expectations. The water washes away and does not hurt the duck. This is a way to avoid getting upset about others' criticism.
- A noxious stimuli is felt (e.g., pain, burning) and at that moment the patient raises his/her head and holds the hand suspended in the air. This symbolizes rising above the negative sensation, to facilitate forbearance.

When used over time, *symbolic gesturing intertwines self-instructions with the gesture* that instructs the person in how to feel and act. In time the gesture stands for the self-talk. For instance, when a patient moves his hand horizontally, he automatically and subconsciously gives himself instructions.

E. OUTCOME ENACTMENT

Solutions-oriented therapy (de Shazer, 1985, 1988, 1991; Selekman, 1999) focuses on times when patients are acting in a way that is part of the desired outcome state. This is referred to as an exception moment, when they are performing actions that are a useful solution for resolving the problem that has brought them to therapy. The treatment rests on encouraging the patient to continue doing what is working, and avoiding actions that do not contribute to the desired outcome state.

Using this idea, CCT asks patients to think of when they are using coping responses that lead to the desired outcome state. For instance, in the case of medical patients, the outcome state may be feeling satisfied with the positive elements of life and not being immersed in what has been lost. The patient is then asked to notice times when s/he is achieving that desired outcome state (referred to as the miracle state, when everything is falling into place). S/he is to take note of what is being done to contribute to that successful outcome. The patient is then asked to continue using that coping response (to do what is already working).

However, if the desired outcome state is not occurring (the miracle has not happened), then the patient is asked to act as if it were happening (Berg and Miller, 1992). S/he is to enact the behaviors and attitude specified in therapy that can lead to the desired outcome state.

F. ENACTING THE ROLE MODEL

This technique uses a role model to stimulate patient behavior. Medical patients are asked to take notice of anyone they have known who handles problems well. Patients are then asked how did they do it? What coping skills does that person possess that allows him/her to act in a productive way? CCT then asks patients to take on the coping responses of that person to achieve the desired outcome state. The patient incorporates those actions by pretending to be the role model when rejection of suffering is detected. The patient leaves his own personality and for a period of time acts as the role model, using his/her positive traits and actions (Sharoff, 2002). Time is spent role-playing the model in general. The patient is encouraged to stay in that role, like an actor. Portions of a day are given over to play-acting that person, at work, in church, visiting others, etc. Another option is having the role model as a mentor. Patients are asked who has been an inspiration to them, or who is someone they respect and admire. They then pretend that the role model is speaking to them in a situation, guiding their actions.

G. ANCHORING

The final tactic uses the Neuro-Linguistic Programming technique of anchoring (Bandler and Grinder, 1975, 1982; King et al., 1983). In this technique, patients first imagine a specific time when they were able to assimilate suffering, when they were able to accept it into their life. To make those situations more vivid, patients can see parts of the scene, smell particular objects in the scene, hear the sounds in the scene, and so on. Then, at the moment the scene is clearly being remembered, the patient touches a particular part of his/her body (e.g., the first knuckle on the right hand). Continuing on, the patient remembers other moments when there was assimilation of suffering and follows the same protocol. Several scenes are remembered and each time the patient touches that same spot. This creates an *anchor to entire positive experiences where the coping skill was employed successfully*. When patients then face a difficult situation in the present, or when experiencing a rejection or suffering, the anchor is used at that moment. The anchor allows patients to rekindle the positive coping moment, which helps them deal with suffering.

Summary

Disallowance of disease can take the form of rejection of suffering. There are various signs of this, including protest against the disease, hatred of it, and the obsessive seeking of a cure. This response needs to be replaced by another that facilitates acceptance of reality, a willingness to bear distress, and forgiveness of the body, oneself, God, fate, or fortune for causing the disease. This response is termed the assimilation of suffering. There are various tactics and techniques to develop assimilation of suffering, including: self-instruction training, imagery, symbolic gesturing, solution-oriented therapy, therapeutic metaphors, becoming the role model, and anchoring.

Chapter 5

Discomfort and Frustration Management

The appearance of noxious, disagreeable, unpleasant physical symptoms cruelly announces the fact that a person's body is not functioning properly. These symptoms are experienced in a variety of ways, perhaps as pain, nausea, throbbing, burning, inflammation, itching, soreness, or a feverish state, but the uniform experience is one of discomfort.

The crisis phase will deepen without an ability to manage physical discomfort. Without specific training in how to manage physical discomfort, patients will feel angry and frustrated because they are unable to eliminate or significantly reduce their discomfort to a "livable level." In that case symptoms will dominate mood and activities, and the impact of disease will be more widespread and injurious than it has to be.

In dealing with physical symptoms, two problems exist. One problem is how to manage unpleasant physical sensations. Two skills are discussed that address that problem. One skill is *discomfort amelioration*, which includes techniques to ease pain and physical discomfort. There is also a need to manage energy to avoid further discomfort. That will require the skill of *energy allocation*. The second problem deals with frustration and anger about having unpleasant sensations that will not go away. Two skills address that issue. One focuses on *frustration tolerance* and the other deals with living with frustration that will not go away. That skill is *frustration accommodation*.

DISCOMFORT MANAGEMENT

Two tactics that are discussed in this section have the modest goal of decreasing physical discomfort, not eradicating it. Patients will still suffer to some extent, which means they will have to use assimilation of suffering techniques as well.

DISCOMFORT AMELIORATION

We will first focus on how to ameliorate the physical discomfort of having symptoms, so symptoms or treatment side effects are less intense. An amelioration strategy seeks to dial down the level of intensity. Once the individual is able to do this, symptoms will drift into the background of daily life experiences. This allows more positive activities to come to the fore. When that occurs, physical symptoms will no longer dominate the perceptual field.

Sensory Diversion Training

The first skill we will study is *sensory diversion training* (Barber, 1977; Scott and Barber, 1977). This technique focuses attention on physical aspects of the environment. It makes use of any of the body's sensory systems to do this. Viewed from a behavioral perspective, it is a *stimulus substitution strategy* (Bandura, 1969). A neutral or pleasant stimulus replaces the negative, noxious, unwanted stimulus (e.g., the bodily symptoms of disease, treatment side effects), which in turn leads to a response other than discomfort, pain, or hurt.

Gestalt psychology supplies an alternative explanation (Koffka, 1935; Kohler, 1947). At any point in time, people perceive a field of images when they look at any given situation. They select only one image and it becomes foreground while all other images in the perceptual field become part of the background. The foreground image shapes the emotional, physical, and behavioral response. An unpleasant foreground image (e.g., fatigue, a burning sensation, pressure) will produce unpleasant feelings. Together, the foreground and background images comprise a gestalt, which means a whole. Sensory diversion training works to replace unpleasant foreground images with neutral or pleasant images. This momentarily creates a neutral to positive effect, in part because the unpleasant image is pushed into the background so it makes less of a negative impact.

Sensory diversion training interferes with or hinders symptoms from dominating the perceptual field. For the patient to gain any benefit from this technique, it will have to become an ongoing mental activity, a discipline regarding the management of painful or noxious stimuli. It will have to be practiced diligently and become a way of life for medical patients beset with physical discomfort. Negative sensations will naturally push to become the dominant foreground image, but the patient must resist that.

Any sense can be used in this technique. If visual diversion is practiced, objects in the perceptual field will be observed. In looking at an object, the eye should trace around each object. For instance, in looking at a chair, the eye can trace along the outer and inner edge of each chair leg. This process continues on and on, as the eye selects one object after another to observe, tracing along the lines of each object. By so doing, neutral to pleasant images replaces stronger, more powerful images (e.g., pain, tingling) that could dominate attention.

In regard to the other senses, for auditory diversion the patient listens to sounds in the room but does not try to identify each sound. Instead, all the sounds are heard like musical notes merging together. Kinesthetic diversion involves noticing bodily sensations that are neutral to pleasant. For instance, someone with low back pain can focus on a nonpainful body part. We will use the right foot as an example. "Note the sensations in the big toe of your right foot, and then move onto the little toe, then the arch of the foot, and the heel of the foot, and so on." Each time a different body part is noticed, a string of temporary Gestalts is formed that are neutral to pleasant, instead of the painful Gestalt that would be formed by focusing on the area in pain. (See disc for handout.)

No-Mind-No-Thing

Frustration is felt when someone responds to something on their mind. A simple answer to this problem is erasing thoughts from the mind. An ancient Zen technique called we-wei or *no-mind-no-thing* does just that (Watts, 1965). It neutralizes hypervigilant searching for threats to well-being and redundant planning seen in the anxious individual. It overcomes the tendency to brood and be preoccupied with past disappointment and loss.

The intent is to quiet the mind by staying in the here and now, respond to what is immediately present, and not shift to the past or future (Sharoff, 2002). There needs to be a willingness to be present to receive the next input. There is only sensory involvement in the situation. Everything is taken in but without special effort. Attention is put on objects without trying to find their meaning. There is an absence of an inner dialogue, and intellectual activity such as problem-solving or deduction is temporarily halted. Reflection on the body's current state or other matters is avoided. The intention is to take the focus off of painful or discomforting stimuli, similar to Sternbach's approach (1978). The body's sensations and condition are experienced along with incoming sensory stimuli, but nothing in particular dominates.

There is a continuous changing of foreground/background images. Immersion into one issue is shunned.

Only short-term goals are pursued. This is termed ***proximal thinking:*** to make plans only to achieve what can be accomplished in the near term. Thinking about long-term goals, called ***distal thinking***, is avoided.

Psychological Distancing

The skill of ***psychological distancing*** helps the patient create a state of psychological distance between him/her and the unpleasant stimulus. Once distant from the stimulus, it makes less of an impact. There are several ways to practice it. (See disc for handout.)

Sensory diversion training is one way to achieve distance. By noticing lines around an object, sounds in the room, or bodily sensations, less attention is paid to other sensations. This simultaneously creates distance from the negative stimuli.

A second technique puts the patient into an ***impartial observer*** role, and observes him/herself from various vantage points. Instruct the patient to see him/herself from rotating angles, such as from across the room, and then from a different location in the room. Or, the patient can become a fly-on-the-wall and see him/herself from one location. An option is viewing the proceedings from behind an imaginary one-way mirror. Patients can perform any action (e.g., take a walk, do the dishes), but mentally they are absorbed into an observer role watching themselves perform an activity. They continue being in pain or experiencing noxious sensations, but by staying in the observer role there is a temporary pulling away from the body, so physical sensations have less of an immediate impact. Afferent nerves signal pain is occurring, but the message is not fully received. The negative physical sensations are still being experienced, but the mind notices them much less.

If discomforting sensations break through and become foreground, make the distancing exercise even more complicated. Have patients see themselves from a different angle in the room. This is now a double removal from self, which complicates the mental state even more and interferes with other mental processes. In this regard, the impartial observer role is also a diversionary tactic.

A third technique puts a patient's life on stage or screen. Real life events become a play or movie, as patients watch themselves and other characters in their lives as an imaginary audience. Patients become actors and their words are now part of a script dialogue. If it is a movie, then patients see the scene from the angle of the camera. To complicate the proceedings even more, patients can talk to themselves in the audience about the movie or play. They can critique their own performance as a medical patient or the performance of other "actors." If physical discomfort builds, continue watching the play, but move on to other imaginary seats in the mental playhouse and see the play from those vantage points.

The patient can vary this technique by becoming a director for the movie. The patient/director moves a mental camera to shoot the scene from different angles, or take close-up shots or distant shots. This complicates the mental activity of watching the situation, and by so doing pulls the patient away from his/her pressing, negative, physical sensations.

Imaginative Transformation

In this technique, the patient's imagination is used to transform an activity that brings about discomfort, which in turn changes effect. A transformation activity can be done in different ways, but essentially the patient alters reality (Turk et al., 1983).

Bodily sensations can be transformed or altered in different ways. For example:

a)   Imagine that the pain in one part of the body has been moved to another part of the body (e.g., the pain in the back is transferred to the right foot).

b)   Imagine a painful part of the body feels different somehow. It now has a pleasant tingling feeling in addition to the other unpleasant physical sensations. Or, it has a new (imaginary) unpleasant physical sensation in the area that hurts in an area that feels no discomfort. By doing that, other sensations are noticed, which create new foreground images. This is an example of a symptom modification technique, where another element is added to the symptom, which causes the latter to be experienced differently (Seltzer, 1986).

c)   Imagine that the entire body has a different feeling, that in general feels relaxing or pleasant. For example, the body feels warm, icy cold, or heavy. The patient proceeds through each part of the body and imagines experiencing that feeling. This is a variation of an autogenics exercise (Schultz and Luthe, 1969).

d) Imagine being in a different context when discomfort is felt. For example, a patient who suffers from a burning sensation in his back imagines standing in a cold, walk-in freezer and feels chilled. All of the body now feels chilled, which moves the focus to other bodily parts as well.

e) Imagine being in a different context but continuing to feel the same discomforting sensations. When this occurs, the same negative physical sensation is experienced differently. For example, a patient with chronic pain from a deteriorating disc is sitting at his desk doing his normal work. He then imagines that he is an undercover detective working at that same job. He is there to gather evidence to bust a group of crooks at his workplace. The patient continues to work but observes the goings-on in the office, as part of being the detective on duty. Even the context for having the back pain can be altered. The patient can imagine getting the back pain while trying to arrest a dangerous crook the previous week. Now the back pain is coming from a heroic struggle.

Self-Instruction Training

Self-talk has been used extensively to ameliorate physical discomfort (Meichenbaum, 1977; Turk et al., 1983). Besides helping patients cope with negative physical states, by supplying an attitude for coexisting with physical discomfort, it also changes the evaluative component of the pain experience. When this happens the pain is experienced as less onerous or hurtful (Melzack, 1965; Melzack and Wall, 1970). For instance, pain once evaluated as unbearable or terrible is now evaluated as undesirable.

When creating the dialogue with the patient, have sentences to prepare a patient for a discomforting activity as well as sentences when first entering the activity and when discomfort peaks. Here is an example of a self-instruction dialogue written for a terminal patient who has substantial physical discomfort and is filled with resentment about dying. He has been asked to engage in daily activities but feels no motivation to do so.

Preparing to Get out of Bed***

I don't want to get out of bed, but I need to. I won't drop out of life while I still have some life left.

Don't get involved with thoughts about life not being fair or it's not right that I'm dying. Life isn't fair but that's reality.

Don't get into bitterness; it will only ruin my day. Overcome my lethargy. I can have more for myself if I get going.

I feel discomfort, but that is my lot in life now. Don't fall into self-pity about it.

Don't focus on my disease.

There are other parts of life to deal with.

Come on. Do it. Get going.

Dealing with Other People

I have to deal with other family members now.

I feel a lot of pain, but I don't want to make my pain their problem. Focus on what these people mean to me. I have little time to be with them. How can I make this moment the best possible?

Don't stay focused on my physical discomfort and sadness about my life ending. I have other times to grieve. Feel the experience of being with my family now. Get into life—not death.

Look carefully at their faces and bodies. Hear their voices. Pay close attention to who they are. Make the moment vivid and intense!

ENERGY ALLOCATION

One of the major causes of discomfort among medical patients is over-commitment and overexertion. Before the onset of symptoms, activities or commitments to engage in an activity could be made easily. But with the advent of disease, life changes drastically for chronic illness patients. Pain, fatigue, and other forms of distress complicate decision making. More time needs to be allocated for job completion; frequent breaks may have to be scheduled. Only part of an activity may be undertaken due to a shortage of energy or physical distress. Suddenly, decisions cannot be made spontaneously. Obligations cannot be undertaken or accepted quickly but must be carefully considered.

The skill of *energy allocation* will help with this matter (Fennell, 2001). It is the ability to organize, plan, and set apart time and physical resources for various activities. It also has a command function by designating what will and will not be done in advance. It gives oneself tasks and refrains from doing other tasks.

Skills for Energy Allocation

The first skills that are required are **self-awareness** and **self-monitoring** (Rehm and Rokhe, 1988). They are self-management techniques. Chronic and terminal illness patients must be able to assess their current physical state, including: pain and fatigue level, energy reserve, and physical tolerance for performing an activity. Judgments must be made and quantified for exactness, such as grading the necessity of performing an action from zero to five, with five being the absolute need for that action. As the activity is undertaken, patients need to become aware if they are overtaxing themselves.

Next, **consequential thinking** is utilized to study and evaluate what consequences can arise from engaging in an activity. To develop this skill, the "what if" question is frequently asked: what problems could arise at various junctures when an activity is undertaken. A decision-tree is helpful in this regard. To adequately deal with problems, **alternative solution thinking** is important to identify other options open to the patient, besides the one others are demanding (Spivack et al., 1976).

To choose the best activity, the skill of **prioritizing** needs to be used to avoid impulsively committing to activities that are too taxing or cause increased pain. To prioritize accurately, **value clarification** is important. Patients have to reorder their values once symptoms arise. Each value has a motivational capacity. Chronic illness patients have to consider the values of the "old self" and realize what values can be retained and what values have to be put aside. **Comparative thinking** will help this process. It weighs one action against another regarding which has more worth to self and others. Prioritizing has to take into consideration others' needs and their value to the patient.

An **objectivity** skill is required when prioritizing, because given the current physical state, the patient has to assign reasonable priorities. The patient has to become aware when guilt or embarrassment factor into decision making. Many medical patients want to do too much to show that "I'm still my old self," and to prove to others "I've still got it." Some do too little in their efforts to save themselves any discomfort and do not challenge themselves enough. To become objective, patients can imagine if they would make the same recommendations for another person as they would make for themselves.

Many activities formerly undertaken by the old self will have to be abandoned or done sparingly, at least when symptoms are intense. This has to be accepted and for this **acceptance training** is important. This entails coming to terms with the reality that certain actions that used to be done can no longer be performed, at least not as much or as regularly as before.

Patients need to install within themselves a gatekeeper function (Fennell, 2001), not to undertake more than is reasonable. The gatekeeper has to guard against being pressured into doing what others want if that will cause a problem. The gatekeeper allows some into the patient's world and keeps others out at various times. The gatekeeper works in accord with values and priorities.

The gatekeeper has to have a wide repertoire of social skills. There needs to be an ability to set limits but in a caring manner, to show empathy to others when disappointing them, and to be able to resolve conflicts amiably. This requires communication training (Gordon, 1970, 1976), *assertiveness training* (Kelly, 1992), and *conflict resolution*. Knowledge of personal rights is helpful for motivating an assertive response (Alberti and Emmons, 1978). To acquire these abilities, the therapist can role-play situations, demonstrate assertive technique, and become the patient's alter ego to identify thinking in various contexts. A counterconditioning format (Bandura, 1969) may need to be developed to grow assertiveness ability.

FRUSTRATION MANAGEMENT

One of the reasons physical discomfort is difficult for people is because they become frustrated. Affectively, people feel discouraged, defeated, and baffled. Physically, people feel tense and aroused; there is a heightened energy with no place to go. Frustration occurs when people feel bad physically and aren't able to stop feeling that way. Medical means to eliminate or reduce discomfort has not succeeded as much as the patient had hoped. Whenever efforts have been thwarted, frustration is felt.

Frustration about symptomatology becomes one of the major effective components of the disease experience. The frustration then becomes part of the affective response to painful physical sensations (Melzack, 1965; Melzack and Wall, 1970). Frustration makes physical pain feel even more painful. Continuing frustration only adds to the level of suffering. Coping with frustration is one of the major challenges facing chronic and terminally ill patients.

In the crisis phase, frustration is extensive because patients are first encountering being thwarted by their disease. They are not used to incursions into their lifestyle. Coping skills have not been adequately developed for managing frustration. This section discusses four skills that can ease the level of frustration: a) frustration tolerance, b) frustration accommodation, c) area thinking, and d) Gestalt management.

FRUSTRATION TOLERANCE

The techniques discussed earlier in the chapter for ameliorating discomfort will lower the level of frustration to some extent but not remove it entirely. Some physical discomfort will still persist, especially if medical solutions are not successful. Faced with some residual level of frustration, a skill is needed to cope with this enervating emotion, and that is *frustration tolerance.*

If patients lack this ability, they will avoid situations that could be beneficial if they simultaneously increase discomfort. Ellis (1979) refers to this as discomfort anxiety, which is fear of situations that will raise the level of discomfort. Discomfort anxiety typically results in avoidance or facing situations with heightened anxiety.

REBT has discussed how a low frustration tolerance is caused by how people think (Ellis and Harper, 1975; Ellis and Grieger, 1979; Wesslers, 1980; Dryden and Ellis, 1988). Cognitive restructuring has been used extensively to change beliefs that lead to heightened frustration. The techniques work to counter irrational, unrealistic beliefs that stimulate frustration and substitutes in their place rational, realistic beliefs that will lead to *less* frustration. With less frustration, people are better able to bear a troublesome situation.

Self-instruction training extends this effort by providing a self-dialogue to inculcate frustration tolerance. Here is a dialogue on tolerating frustration when there are bodily symptoms.

SELF-TALK TO TOLERATE FRUSTRATION***

My body is not working the way that I want.

I don't like this situation, but I can stand things not going my way.

I can cope with the frustration from having physical discomfort.

I would prefer not being frustrated by these symptoms, but that comes with having a chronic (or terminal) illness.

No one has said life will be easy. Having a chronic (or terminal) illness is not easy, but I can bear up.

Discomfort is a result of my disease. Accept it. Bear it. Live with it.

When I get upset, just relax. Take a few deep breaths.

Don't make demands on my body that it cannot meet. That will only cause more frustration.

Think of other times when I tolerated frustration during my illness. I can do the same now.

To reflexively say these statements, *cognitive rehearsal* is utilized. The patient repeats this dialogue several times a day, and then repeats sentences when dealing with bodily symptoms. In addition, other subskills can facilitate or aid frustration tolerance. *Problem-solving* (Goldfried and Merbaum, 1973; Spivack et al., 1976; Mahoney, 1977) is helpful to find ways to achieve desired goals, and by doing so there is less frustration. For example, patients experiencing pain or fatigue will have to find alternative ways to fulfill role duties. They will need to be aware of the consequences of a particular action, so they can avoid increased pain or exhaustion. *Consequential thinking* is enlisted for this purpose. *Relaxation training* (Jacobson, 1972; Benson, 1975) is quite useful for decreasing stress and anger that accompanies frustration. Relaxation eases muscle tension that causes inflammation, which in turn increases the level of pain. *Self-monitoring* is used in conjunction with relaxation to note excessive amounts of frustration. A high level of frustration will cue the use of relaxation or self-instructions. Afterwards, self-evaluation can rate the effectiveness of these skills.

Symbolic gesturing can be used to facilitate frustration tolerance. For example, a patient can take a deep breath and raise his forearm. This symbolizes an increase in frustration. As he exhales he lowers his forearm, to symbolize a lowering of frustration by practicing frustration tolerance. At the same time the breath is exhaled, self-talk phrases can be repeated, such as, "Let it go. Give it up. Out of body." ("It" is frustration.)

Imagery can be used to tolerate frustration. For example, patients can imagine a strong wind (standing for frustration from any stressor) is blowing against them, but they do not mind the wind because they are wearing a sturdy windbreaker (standing for frustration tolerance) that protects against the chill. They stand against the wind formidably, because they know that they can tolerate it.

FRUSTRATION ACCOMMODATION

Compared with the premorbid state, medical patients with symptomatology usually have far more difficulty performing the activities of daily living. For example, many arthritis patients find difficulty just opening a jar or buttoning a shirt. If there is disability, then patients have to face performance decrement and inevitable frustration. The medical patient also suffers frustration dealing with other people's frustrations.

After a while many patients become disgusted with being so frustrated so much of the time! They reject having to tolerate a sustained level of frustration in their daily lives, but that response only heightens their level of frustration. They have frustration about being frustrated (Dryden and Ellis, 1988). Instead, they need the skill of *frustration accommodation*, an ability to create a mind-set that allows not only for an increase in frustration but also its on-going presence.

Frustration tolerance is different from frustration accommodation. The former is an ability to bear or withstand frustration or distress that arises while performing tasks. People with a low frustration tolerance will need to practice that skill. Frustration accommodation is a response that allows for and contains frustration as a common and inevitable part of a medical patient's daily life. It treats the secondary problem of becoming frustrated because of frequent frustration. Medical patients who reject frustration in their life will need to practice frustration accommodation first and then move on to using frustration tolerance.

Self-instruction training is one way to inculcate frustration accommodation. It emphasizes acceptance.

SELF-TALK PRIOR TO AN ACTIVITY THAT WILL BE FRUSTRATING***

I have to do something that may increase my frustration.

I will have to put up with it. I can live with an increase in frustration.

I have coped in other situations, and I can here as well.

Having a chronic illness means more frustration in my daily life and that's the way it is. That comes with the territory of my disease.

Accept the fact that my activities will be more difficult to perform.

SELF-TALK WHEN BECOMING FRUSTRATED

I'm becoming frustrated because I don't like being frustrated.

I can cope with a life of frustration if I so choose. When I do, I will not feel so distressed. I can manage my emotions.

Frustration is part of my existence now. Allow for it. Make room for it.

Don't start hating the difficulties of performing tasks. That will only make them harder to tolerate.

I cannot do things as easily as I used to. Accept that fact.

Frustration accommodation is a response substitution strategy. The patient identifies situations where s/he may feel frustrated and then practices a tactic such as self-talk to accommodate to frustration in that context.

AREA THINKING

One reason chronic and terminally ill patients feel frustrated is that they select goals that cannot be achieved. Medical patients are routinely forced to make decisions about what they can achieve, given their physical limitations. If they select unachievable goals, they will be more frustrated when they have disappointing results. To choose achievable goals, they will need the skill of *area thinking* (Sharoff, 2002).

Let's examine how area thinking will work with medical patients. Suppose a patient has the goal of achieving a cure. That is a goal that cannot be achieved by the patient, because it is affected by numerous external factors such as the competency of the health provider, the provider's treatment plans, anatomical condition, genetic susceptibility, relative efficacy of medication with that person, and organ response to treatment. Hence, cure is largely outside a patient's area of influence. What goals can be pursued by the patient regarding the issue of cure? He/she can attend physical therapy, eat, and exercise according to the medical regimen. He can select a goal of getting enough rest, securing medical facts that can alleviate anxiety, or choose another doctor. All of these pursuits are within a patient's area of influence. However, none of them can directly bring about a cure. The patient, though, has to be content with "working his/her area." If that brings about a goal external to him/her, that is great, but there is no guarantee of that occurring when a goal is outside someone's area of influence. If patients are upset about not being cured, then they are angry that they are unable to control forces beyond their own area of influence. They are upset about not having ultimate or omnipotent power.

In summary, if patients do not want to be frustrated more than they have to be, they should only select goals that are within their area of influence. Area thinking helps to select activities that can lead to attainable goals. Area thinking works in tandem with **acceptance training**. The acceptance response is practiced to develop readiness to live with the inability to control forces beyond the individual. It helps to develop admission of and allowance for personal limitation, and willingness to coexist with limitations. Acceptance utilizes realistic thinking to carefully appraise what the individual can and cannot affect.

Another component of area thinking involves the selection of behavior. There are two behavioral choices open to people: choose a surrender strategy or a nonsurrender strategy. For instance, a nonsurrender strategy may involve taking medication in the hope that it will lead to a remission of symptoms, or proceeding with surgery or therapy. A surrender strategy may involve not pursuing efforts for an eventual cure (e.g., refusing surgery or further treatment). Another facet of area thinking is knowing *when* to surrender, *when not* to surrender, or *when* surrender is inevitable. For instance, terminal patients need to know when to stop seeking a cure and become ready to surrender to death.

Another component of area thinking is *prioritizing*. Medical patients need to know which is the most important goal to pursue at that moment in time. For instance, a patient can emphasize seeking a cure, focusing on complying with the medical regimen, or coping with symptoms. When a cure is not realized or the regimen does not lead to relief, then coping needs to become the more important goal at that moment. Priorities will shift over time. Part of area thinking is selecting the best outcome to pursue among several alternatives for a given time period.

Steps in performing area thinking:

1) Select an outcome that is within one's capacity to achieve.
2) Assess if the outcome is outside one's area of influence.
3) If the goal is outside of a person's area, then acceptance needs to be employed to change thinking that a given goal should not be pursued.
4) Prioritize the most important goal in a given context.
5) Select the strategy for accomplishing the goal: a surrender or non-surrender strategy.
6) If a nonsurrender strategy is selected, then use problem-solving to think of other ways to achieve a goal. Plot the tactics to reach the goal.

GESTALT MANAGEMENT

The fourth subskill of frustration management is a perceptual skill, the ability to select and experience a foreground image that leads to positive feelings or minimum negative feelings. In this technique, medical patients struggling with frustration are trained to be in charge of their perceptual process. This is the skill of **Gestalt management** (Perls et al., 1951).

People have two important tasks regarding a Gestalt: a) select a foreground image to attend to, and b) experience that foreground image to some extent (Polsters, 1973; Zinker, 1977). Gestalt management becomes involved in these two tasks in different ways.

It can substitute one Gestalt for another. Foreground image selection can be done mindlessly and subconsciously, or deliberately and consciously. Patients with a disease have a tendency to automatically focus on physical problems or the losses that stem from symptoms. The subconscious process mindlessly focuses on what has gone wrong, what is lacking, and what hurts. If this occurs, the foreground image will be on negative matters. Oppositely, people can consciously, deliberately manage their Gestalts and choose those that will result in a neutral or positive end state.

Sensory diversion training works to do this. For instance, when feeling nervous talking to a doctor, a patient can switch the foreground image to a neutral image (e.g., the cleanliness of the doctor's office).

Another tactic uses a "ritual Gestalt." Whenever someone is stressed they can ritualistically focus on another foreground image from the past (e.g., their childhood bed). Another way to facilitate a ritual Gestalt is by using the Neuro-Linguistic Programming technique of an anchor (King et al., 1983). A past self image is remembered when there was a feeling of peace and calm, and at that moment a particular body part is touched (e.g., the second knuckle of the right hand). Whenever feeling frustrated, a patient can touch that body part, rekindling that old image from the past. A third use of a ritual Gestalt utilizes an image of the goal state, where a person is acting out the solutions that will lead to goal attainment. The image is formed when there is frustration, to lead someone to install solution behavior. This tactic uses ideas from solution-oriented therapy (de Shazer, 1988).

Another aspect of Gestalt management concerns the experiencing of a foreground image. A Gestalt can have more or less of an effect on mood and thinking, depending on how deeply it is experienced. For example, a medical patient has an experience that turns out well because of his efforts. He feels capable. However, if that feeling is not experienced vividly then it will be lost or not make an impact. The positive effect on self-esteem and self-concept will be minimal. Gestalt management has patients experience positive moments fully.

To do so:

a) focus on something positive (e.g., an achievement)
b) give attention to the experience (a feeling of victory)
c) savor the experience by feeling it intensely
d) prolong the positive feelings by vividly noticing all facets of the experience.
e) at various times of the day repeat steps a) through d) to refire the positive experience in memory.

Summary

Physical discomfort is one of the hallmarks of disease. Ameliorating discomfort can be achieved by sensory diversion, the tactic of no-mind-no-thing, psychological distancing, and imaginative transformation. Self-instruction training is helpful for that purpose as well. Frustration is an emotion that makes physical discomfort more unpleasant. Frustration management is needed, and it involves frustration tolerance, frustration accommodation, area thinking, and Gestalt management. An energy allocation ability will decrease physical discomfort.

Chapter 6

Identity Management

> "I tell my kids, 'Dad is dead.' I cannot be my old self. He's gone. They shouldn't look to me to be 'Dad' anymore."
> —Jamie, low back pain patient

As symptoms arise in the crisis stage, patients encounter an inconsistency between self-image and present functioning: "This is not me. Who is this new me?" Former characteristic behavior does not match present behavior. The historical self-concept is incongruent with present images of self. Chronic and terminal illness patients suddenly find that the person they have become is not the person they once were. Self-alienation arises regarding the new form of self, which does not represent the known individual. What's more, the new self, the new identity, is not very well liked, even abhorred.

Throughout the disease process, identities will continue to be challenged and altered. Both the chronically and terminally ill face the same difficulty: how to maintain identity in a shifting world. Symptoms and the treatment for those symptoms change roles and behaviors that formerly supported and developed identity. The resulting identity crisis is one of the most significant issues facing medical patients. It is a prime contributor to depression and suicidal urge. How medical patients will deal with this crisis is a vital part of treatment.

This chapter discusses ways to treat identity crisis, by developing the skill of *identity management*. It addresses the problem of how to maintain identity and redefine oneself. Identity management requires two sub-skills: *image scrutiny* and *identity coalescing*.

WHAT IS IDENTITY?

Identity is a subtle yet powerful entity. It is usually taken for granted until it is lost. Identity is the collective aspect of the characteristics by which people recognize themselves. These characteristics can be repetitive thoughts and attitudes, recurring actions, or traits. By frequently performing various actions or thinking certain thoughts, people come to define who they are. Moreover, those characteristics create continuity. Identity reaffirms that we are the same and a persisting entity (e.g., healthy, robust, strong, virile), which allows us to take ourselves for granted, in a positive way.

Identity is intrinsically involved with the structure of concepts. All concepts are defined by their relevant features (Rosch, 1973, 1975). The best example of a feature is the prototype, which illustrates the concept. There are prototypical features that are salient so they stand out in people's minds. The prototype becomes the core meaning for the concept, or the self-concept in the case of identity. A prototype feature can even represent the category (identity) because it is so dominant in people's minds. Everyone naturally formulates their relevant, prototypical features that become part of their identity.

With symptom onset, new features are added to identity and they, too, become defining features. Because disease features are so dominant in the crisis phase, they become prototypes that define the medical patient. For example, because death is so dominant in a person's mind, being a "dying" person becomes the prototypical feature of the terminally ill patient. Likewise, "total disability" and "inability to work" can become prototypical features. They are such strong features of the concept (the concept in this case is the self) that they drive out other features. Other features' degree of category membership (the membership of features that comprise identity) is reduced or eliminated. For example, in the chronically fatigued patient, the features "vigorous" and "robust" lose category membership when defining identity.

While role functioning develops identity, once identity is formed it can either facilitate further role functioning or end it. For example, once a fatigued patient assumes the identity of a haggard individual, he will avoid role commitments, fearing they will not be fulfilled. Oppositely, because of identity, people will make a commitment to others, knowing that they can perform an action ("I am energetic, so I can take that on.").

Identity allows people to become part of a group, and that buttresses self-esteem. For example, before symptom onset, Daryl enjoyed membership in the group of "strong, powerful, tough people." But after symptom onset, he felt chronically fatigued and uncoordinated. Muscles felt weak and his gait was insecure. He lost membership in the group that supported his identity and instead gained membership in a group that he disliked: the infirm and unsteady. He experienced an obliteration of self that both frightened and infuriated him. He felt helpless watching who he was and whom he valued vanish before his eyes.

In general, asymptomatic patients experience less identity crisis because their symptoms do not impinge on role functioning as much as with symptomatic patients. But as chronic illness drags on, the asymptomatic patient also has to address this issue sooner or later. Unwillingness to address identity changes will directly affect compliance to the medical regimen.

TYPES OF IDENTITY CRISIS

There are three simultaneous identity processes in medical patients: *identity adulteration, identity alienation, and identity loss.* Identity adulteration occurs when self-image is not only altered but sullied in the person's eyes and there is dislike of the new identity, which spoils the former image of self. Accompanying this is a reduction in self-esteem. Said in a different way, if a feature (e.g., energetic, sure-footed, powerful gait) no longer bears a family resemblance to other members in the same category (e.g., unsteady walk, weak limbs), then that feature has been adulterated (Rosch and Mervis, 1975). For instance, formerly energetic people who prized their vitality, experience identity adulteration when they develop a disease that causes fatigue.

The choices that medical patients are forced to make contribute to identity adulteration. Continuing with the example of fatigue, a patient may have to choose between "I can wash my hair or I can wash the dishes but I cannot do both. Which shall I pick?" The inability to do both forces the medical patient to concede that the prototypical feature "energetic" is no longer applicable.

A cognitive activity, reductionistic thinking, contributes to identity adulteration. An equivalency is made in someone's mind: I am equal to this limited set of traits (e.g., weak, unsteady limbs). The totality of that person is then reduced to that set of traits. Reductionistic thinking may have worked on the patient's behalf before the onset of symptoms ("I am beautiful") but afterward it works against her ("I am disfigured and ugly").

The disease and the treatment for it inadvertently create new images of self that are not wanted, causing alienation toward that new self. *Identity alienation is an unfriendliness and indifference toward the new self* beset by bodily dysfunction. It is also a way to cope with the new self. The estrangement allows a person to disown who he/she has become. The self, affected by disease and treatment, is then looked at as someone else—the not-me state—who aches, looks different, cannot complete role duties, and upsets other people. This is a type of dissociation, where a patient refuses to associate with who s/he has become. By not identifying with the new self, there is less anger against it.

At the same time, identity alienation is a way to preserve the old identity. There is a real me, the good me, the old me. I am different from this bad me, the diseased me, who does not represent the real me. The self-recrimination is not directed against the real me but the diseased me who is not part of self.

However, there are limits to this strategy and it cannot go on for long. Sooner or later the self must see who s/he has become, and at that point *identity loss* is felt. Certain features of a concept (identity) will always be favored over others. When favored features are eliminated from a concept, identity loss is felt. This is a cognitive-affective state. There is intellectual recognition that a feature has been eliminated from category membership, and there is anguish and sadness because some sacred and prized part of the self has been lost or severely damaged.

For example, breasts are a prototypical feature of the category "woman." Wendy, a mastectomy patient, no longer thought of herself as feminine or womanly because she had lost that prototypical feature. Her breasts were a central tendency feature. With reconstructive surgery she felt the return of her breast as a prototypical, womanly feature, and her sadness over identity loss eased substantially.

Some women, though, still feel identity loss after reconstructive surgery. That is because there are allowable variations within a category regarding features (Rosch, 1975). Some features can vary from the defining features to some degree. In the minds of some women, the breast implants varied too much within the category of breasts. Hence, the example of the prototype (the reconstructed breasts) were eliminated from the category (of allowable examples of breasts).

Identity loss becomes more evident when activities have to be surrendered that supported identity and imparted a sense of self. With the loss of those activities, the self feels depleted. There are insufficient positive activities to support a rich enough view of self.

Suzanne provides a case example of all three identity crises. She viewed herself as a sexy, desirable woman who pleased her partner in bed. She saw herself as someone possessing a strong sex drive, and she liked how her body performed during sex. This was a dominant part of her self-image and this view supported her self-esteem. Then, in her early thirties, she developed multiple sclerosis that caused her to feel fatigued, which in turn decreased her interest in sex.

Achieving orgasm became difficult because of impaired sensation. Many coitus positions became difficult for her. Most frustrating for her though, was the problem of urinary incontinence during coitus. Other problems diminished her overall view of herself as an attractive woman: her spasticity, nystagmus, a slight tremor, clumsiness, and loss of muscular coordination. She knew that she was not nearly as physically desirable to her husband anymore.

She found herself feeling ashamed of whom she was sexually (identity adulteration). She did not want to see who she had become (identity alienation). She apologized to her husband profusely when she did not feel like having sex ("This is not me. I don't know what's wrong with me!"), and felt ashamed of her urinary problems. A deep sadness engulfed her when she remembered who she had been sexually before her disease struck (identity loss). That person was now gone, and she grieved for her.

TREATMENT CONSIDERATIONS

There are superordinate categories (e.g., male) that are the broadest abstract levels for a category (Rosch et al., 1976). Other features of the category must define it because it's too broad of a term. Under that superordinate category there are basic levels of the category that further define the concept (e.g., working person, muscular, powerful, strong, tough, durable). Disease causes some basic-level characteristics to be lost. A therapist has two choices. One is to reinstall a basic-level characteristic, so it stays within that category. This can be done by **reframing** that characteristic, so it can be viewed from a different perspective. The second is for the therapist to find other basic characteristics that allow a person to remain a part of the superordinate category. Either strategy allows a patient to regain category membership. In general, there is a need to hold favored features within that category as much as possible, and to maintain favored category membership as long as possible.

In the treatment of Daryl, a multiple sclerosis patient, the therapist used the first strategy. Daryl felt less like a man (a superordinate category) because he lost some basic, prototypical, or central tendency features of that category. He was no longer powerful and strong in movement. He felt expelled from the category of "male" as a consequence. The therapist worked to preserve prototypical features of that category. He described Daryl as tough and durable (other common basic characteristics of the superordinate category) because he withstood his disease and carried on role duties at home. This reframed the idea of tough, and reinstalled and bolstered Daryl's membership in the male category.

In the treatment of Wendy, her therapist used the second strategy. He described how Wendy has other basic features of the superordinate category "woman" or "feminine." The therapist described her as gentle, nurturing, and caring. This expanded the category of woman in her mind, recently diminished after her breast surgery. While she lost a prototypical feature (her breasts) she still had many other basic-level features that certainly preserved her category membership.

IMAGE SCRUTINY

After symptoms begin to emerge, and after the diagnosis has been given to the patient, individuals may either continue relating to chronic and terminal patients as they had in the past, or begin relating much differently. That new way of relating will give patients new images of themselves, some positive and some negative. For example, the patient may now be seen as trouble, a burden, a nuisance, a malingerer, or deceitful. Each image is a pejorative view of self. Further, some diseases may not be accepted as an authentic illness, such as fibromyalgia or chronic fatigue syndrome. Patients receiving that diagnosis may be mistrusted, and that will become a new image for the patient. At the same time, patients give themselves new and negative images as a consequence of the disease or its treatment.

The images that others have of the patient, and the images patients have of themselves, constitute feedback. That feedback can be given directly and verbally ("I'm really unhappy with you."), or indirectly and nonverbally (e.g., through cold stares, sneers, raised eyebrows, or deep sighs). To illustrate: after Beth's husband died she took over the family finances. She received feedback from his parents in the form of disbelieving expressions that she could not do this job. Nonverbally they saw her as a boob. When Beth did not grasp complicated matters about her husband's retirement funds, she became exasperated, providing another self-image that she was "not too quick."

In summary, patients are barraged with multiple images of self. These images are taken in mostly on an unconscious level, but they shape identity profoundly. To avoid incorporating a negative, unwarranted self-image, chronic and terminally ill patients need to develop the skill of *image scrutiny*.

This is an ability to self-question, to carefully examine and study transmitted images for accuracy. It involves a capacity to give close observation to each image by collecting data to determine if that image fits oneself. The purpose is twofold: a) to increase self-awareness of images foisted on oneself, by either the individual or others, and b) to assess if that image is justified, based on knowledge of oneself or the facts in the situation. Medical patients are advised to engage in image scrutiny regularly, especially after a conflict with someone or when feeling negatively about oneself.

These are some questions that need to be asked after a self-representation is identified. See disc for questionnaires.

- Is the self-image I now have of myself the way I think of myself in general?
- Is there reason to start thinking of myself this way? Should I change my general or long-term image of myself to match this present view of self?
- If I continue to think of myself this way, what would be the consequences? What will I gain or lose by thinking of myself this way?
- Is this view of myself warranted? What facts support this view? Have I done anything to merit this view?
- Where did I get this view? From myself or another person? Have I had this view before? Was it warranted at those times?
- Am I falling into an old way of thinking of myself? Were those past ideas justified? Am I thinking of myself now as I thought of myself when I was a child?
- If I do not like this view of me, and it is not warranted, what can I do to rid myself of this self-representation?
- If I do not like this view of me and it is warranted, what can I do to change this view of me? How would I have to act differently?

After images of self have been evaluated, the patient moves onto the next task of **deciding if the image should be incorporated into his or her identity.** This is a choice to reject or accept a view of self. If the image of self is negative but accurate, then patients have to know how to handle that information so it is not overwhelming, does not result in defensiveness, or hurts a relationship with another person who gives the information.

Medical patients need to know how to deal with true but hurtful images of self. To address this issue, the skill of **relabeling** is helpful (Seltzer, 1986; Weeks and L'Abate, 1982). This is an ability to find another word that can describe the same set of facts. The new word fits the facts but changes how they are perceived. The alternative label gives a positive image to the situation, which helps to preserve or build self-esteem. It allows people to make a conceptual shift (McMullin, 1986), without having to formally dispute the term as in the case of cognitive restructuring. For example, *slow* can be relabeled as *deliberate and careful* work.

IDENTITY COALESCING

Having a chronic or terminal illness dramatically reshapes identity. Some will think of themselves as victims while others will see themselves as heroes or heroines struggling against overwhelming odds. Roles are often altered or lost when a disease occurs and this, too, will change identity. This gives chronic and terminally ill patients the task of designing a new identity, based on old and new roles, traits, images, and ways of functioning. That task requires the skill of *identity coalescing*.

Several tasks must be performed to acquire this skill. First, there is a need to blend both old and new identities. This involves the skill of *weighting*. Patients need to be careful not to ignore old traits when barraged by new, negative images of self, or give too much weight to new qualities or changes in self that are a result of the disease. Past abilities still in operation may not be given enough weight because present inability prejudices the view of self. For example, Ralph, a cancer patient, saw himself as the owner of a rotting body. He mostly considered himself disease ridden and inadequate. Other images of self were not allowed to surface. There were many days when he functioned better than others, but his self-view remained stuck on negative self-images. Although incapacitated to some degree by his cancer and the treatment for it, he also had many other capacities that he did not consider.

Second, the blending of old and new qualities and capacities has to be a constant and continuous task. One image of self can become foreground too much of the time while other images are relegated and pushed into the background, thus skewing self-concept. Unlike healthy individuals, a medical patient can be different every day, depending on factors such as weather, degree of symptomatology, and willingness to follow the treatment regimen. Therefore, patients need to reform their identity daily, depending on how they are doing.

A third task is avoiding value judgments as much as possible. Value judgements emerge as salient and are more influential than descriptive judgments. They dominate experiences and individuals respond to them quickly. To inhibit them, the skill of *evaluative restraint* is needed. It inhibits and sidetracks the tendency to editorialize, critique, and rate. It uses an internal censor to identify value judgments and suspend their use.

In place of evaluative judgments, *descriptive judgments* are promoted. Using empirical data, they simply record what is occurring or how something looks. Sensory based language is used to describe a condition, manner, behavior, or internal activity. They do not condemn, criticize, or rate. They capture elements of the experience without lowering self-esteem. They give a nonprejudiced view of appearance or role performance.

A fourth task involves acting without standards. Standards can have a pernicious effect on medical patients. Because medical patients often have difficulty meeting past standards, maintaining them inevitably damages self-esteem. For example, Ruth, a mastectomy patient receiving chemotherapy and radiation, sees her bald head in the mirror, and the first thing she thinks about is not measuring up to "normal" standards of beauty. She thinks about her mastectomy and immediately thinks of the standard for women who are equipped with two breasts. Hence, her identity is adulterated by what she has lost. While standards cannot be avoided entirely, suspending standards allows someone to relate to an experience as it is and not how it is supposed to be. In place of standards, goals are set that realistically appraise what the patient can do. *Area thinking* influences which goals are selected. Only goals within someone's area of influence are chosen.

Once standards are set aside, patients can attend to other facets of the situation that can bolster self-esteem or offer a new way to perform an activity. For example, Beth is chronically fatigued and has muscle weakness. She cannot make as many calls as she used to because of her condition. Yet, her company accepts her current output as adequate even though Beth thinks only about not meeting standards for her position as she used to. However, when Beth does not evaluate her output and drops her standards, she feels better. She simply describes her actions to learn how she can change her job performance (e.g., "I related well to this client but could have emphasized that point more strongly with this other one.")

SUMMARY

An important treatment task in the crisis phase is the reconstruction of identity that is altered with the advent of disease. Identity is defined as the features that characterize the self. There are three important identity crises: identity adulteration, identity alienation, and identity loss. Therapists need to know how to preserve positive identity and minimize identity loss. Once someone becomes a medical patient, he/ she will receive many images of self. Patients need to be trained to scrutinize the incoming images. Another basic treatment task is bringing together an identity that encapsulates the old and new identity. This is referred to as identity coalescing.

Chapter 7

Self-Support Training

> I get down on myself so quickly because I know I am not as productive as the other workers. I sure can be hard on myself.
> —Kathy, fibromyalgia patient

When symptoms first arise in the crises phase, some individuals feel impatient about not being able to be their old self. They respond with self-criticism instead of offering themselves aid and encouragement. There are others who find their spirits slipping with the advent of disease and are not able to endure or tolerate their health problems on their own. To prevent themselves from sinking into despair, they need the caring approval of others. Problems arise though, when family, friends, or coworkers are too frustrated with the patient to give approval. Others receive support from others, but it is given inconsistently. Those patients cannot rely on those closest to them. In addition, there are many people who are generally not supportive. While physically and psychologically hurting and needing self-compassion, they are not even able to give that to themselves.

Many medical patients find themselves suffering from a lack of support at a time when they need it the most. This only adds to their feeling of crisis. Instead, they need to develop a self-support capacity that can be relied upon when external support lacking or insufficient. This chapter discusses how to build that ability.

Cognitive restructuring (CR) is helpful for removing non-supportive behavior, such as hypercriticalness and self-derision due to inflexible, unreasonable expectations. CR may create realistic standards that can be met, which indirectly leads to self-approval. However, CR does not directly build the self-support response. CR does not guarantee a replenishing of lost pride, behavior that boosts self-esteem, and actions that can soothe hurt or fear. CR does not necessarily create a capacity for reassurance and self-encouragement when those qualities are generally lacking. It may not make patients into an advocate for themselves when they most need one.

A more concentrated effort focusing on constructing self-support capacity is required. *Self-support training* has four component subskills. One is to become a *self-booster*, the behavioral capacity to boost self-esteem and self-confidence. The second sub-skill is *self-compassion*, the ability to relate to self in a warm, caring, nurturing way. The third is *self-advocacy*, the ability to defend the self against self-attack or attack by others. A fourth skill, exoneration training, overcomes self-punitive, self-critical behavior and guilt-provoking thinking. (See coping skills manual for check-off form to inculcate these self-support skills.)

SELF-BOOSTER TRAINING

Self-booster training works to develop a habitual response that overemphasizes the good and underemphasizes the bad in oneself. It is a cognitive-perceptual activity. Cognitively, patients think about their abilities while overlooking personal shortcomings. The cognitive distortion of mental filtering aids this effort by preserving the good and eliminating the bad in oneself. It notes daily victories and remembers routine achievements while filtering out defeats. Disappointing behavior that does not meet personal standards is ignored. More weight is given to positive components of performance while offering a rationale for negative job performance. Self-reinforcement is stressed; compliments and self-praise are given freely and effusively. Self-criticism is shunned. There is an extensive use of the phrase, "I like how I . . . " The intention is to make a "big to-do" about what has been attained. Essentially, self-boosting trains patients to skew the data and not be objective when looking at themselves. See disc for patient questionnaire.

This activity goes against a basic tenet of cognitive therapy that promotes realistic thinking. So why is it being promoted? The reason is that illness or infirmity creates a preponderance of negative views of self. Disease limits what the self can do well or used to do well. It precludes activities that were the foundation for a healthy self-image. It chips away at self-esteem. Self-boosterism compensates for this problem by tilting the scale, weighed down by negative self-perceptions, in favor of positive views of self. It restores self-confidence and encourages an image that the patient is or can be adept, given the medical problem that limits effort and achievement.

In other words, there are times when being realistic creates a problem and hinders self-growth. The crisis phase is one of those times when incapacity is prominent. At that time a heavy dose of praise, admiration, and self-regard is needed. Later, when feeling better about themselves, patients can resume being objective and realistic.

To induce the patient to become a self-booster, there must first be a discussion about the need for this activity and how it can aid the medical intervention. Patients need to understand the mind-body connection, to realize that physiological systems are sensitive to the influence of the central nervous system, and psychological matters in particular (Selye, 1976; Cox, 1979). Specifically, the immune system acts as a mediator between the effects of psychosocial factors (e.g., self-derision) and the precipitation and perpetuation of a variety of diseases (Ader and Cohen, 1984). The lack of self-support is one key stressor that taxes the immune system.

Once there is more motivation to be self-supportive, therapists should inquire how patients generally attempt to support themselves. If it is lacking, then this problem must be brought to the attention of the patient. To increase interest in being self-supportive, inquire if the patient knows anyone whom s/he likes and respects and is known to be a self-supportive individual. This will create a positive role model.

Next, patients need to be asked if there is anything that could cause them to resist being self-supporting. For instance, could anger at themselves cause them to withhold it? If they are not a generally supportive person, does rigidity of personality prevent them from acting out of character? The treatment of resistance to self-support will be a primary treatment matter.

For some patients, a simple explanation giving the rationale for self-boosting is enough to encourage that activity. Others who are not generally self-supportive will need a more concentrated effort. They will have to structure their time to include self-boosting. Self-complimentary sessions will have to be scheduled throughout the day. They are termed "liking sessions." To show that they bring results, have the patient rate how they feel before and after each session.

The format for a liking session is as follows. The patient writes down what was done during a given time period and then rates how well that task was done. This is a mastery rating (Beck et al., 1979). Whatever aspects of the task that were done well are noted and enjoyed. Discourage comparing the performance to premorbid functioning. Encourage the patient to momentarily hold the achievement in view, to make it foreground, so it can be savored even more. As this is being done the patient says the phrase, "I like how I did . . . "

A liking session can be enhanced by transforming it into a celebration. The patient can gather some favorite foods and beverages and then phone or sit with significant others to talk about daily accomplishments. The patient and others "toast" these accomplishments, so it is a "hooray" activity! For special accomplishments, the patient can give him/herself a gift as a reward. Encourage patients that *measured bragging* about what they have attained is productive.

At the same time, medical patients may have to train significant others in how to be a supportive. First, patients will need the *self-awareness* ability to pinpoint their needs. Second, they will need communication skill to motivate others to be supportive. Patients who are passive and have difficulty doing this will require *assertiveness training* (Jakubowski and Lange, 1973), which includes commendatory assertiveness (Kelly, 1982). If others do not respond as desired, *forgiveness training* is needed to quickly dissipate anger (Sharoff, 2002). Self-instruction training for anger management can supplement this (Meichenbaum, 1977). Knowledge of beliefs that promote anger is also helpful (Ellis, 1977).

SELF-COMPASSION TRAINING

In the last section, the role of the self-booster was discussed. This section discusses how to perform that role. It calls for a special self-response that shows warmth and caring, gives comfort, extends empathy, and soothes when feeling distressed. This is the skill of *self-compassion*. Therapists can use the term from Transactional Analysis of a *nurturing* parent when explaining self-boosting and self-compassion training to patients. The nurturing parent develops a capacity within the patient to limit the pernicious effects of the frustrated *critical parent,* who may have become oversized when symptoms precluded normal role functioning (Berne, 1961; Harris, 1967).

Because medical patients face major obstacles and have had such extensive losses, they need a loving, uplifting way of relating to themselves. Self-compassion substitutes for other people who may not be able or willing to provide that response, either because they are not capable of offering it, or are disinclined to offer it due to their own anger at the patient for depriving them of what they want. (In the latter case, support is withheld to punish the patient.) Given that, a reliable source for securing compassion needs to be developed, and it should start with the patient.

What are the facets of self-compassion?

A. ***Permission giving:*** This self-interactive activity offers consent and allows one ***not to act in certain ways.*** In essence the patient is excused from meeting the expectations of family, employer, friends, peer group, or reference group, when it is not possible to do so. Further, patients are excused from meeting their own expectations. For example, permission is given to look less than one's best, to perform below one's abilities, to leave a production incomplete, or not care for others when not feeling up to it. Parents are excused from being a service provider for their children. The act of permission-giving makes allowances for inadequacy caused by the disease or the treatment for it. It modifies role requisites and standards, so they are reasonable, given the patient's condition of the moment. Quite commonly, permission is given to create more lenient self-standards (e.g., relax normal hygiene standards or time demands for task completion). Permission-giving grants the excuse that is needed to avoid or expunge guilt or self-recrimination. (The self-compassion activity is designed for patients who are motivated to fulfill expectations and meet standards but cannot due to their condition. It certainly can be taken advantage of by medical patients known as malingerers. They have a lack of motivation and are able to fulfill role expectations but are unwilling to do so.)

B. ***Mercy:*** Self-compassion training seeks to develop a merciful way of relating to oneself, especially when engaging in permission-giving. It is promoted to overcome the self-disdain that many chronic illness patients have developed. Mercy extends forgiveness and kindness to oneself.

C. ***Soft-heartedness:*** This is a behavioral activity where the patient relates to him/herself in a tender, gentle way, with grace, forbearance, and sympathy. The self-compassion response seeks a softness, especially when behavior does not meet the norm, when chronic or terminal illness lessens competency and potency.

The goal is to build an overall response capacity that includes these responses when encountering negative stimuli (e.g., symptoms of fatigue, disfigurement, or bodily weakness). There is also an intention to use self-compassion as a response substitution for impatience, frustration with self, and self-pity.

Self-pity is a form of self-compassion. When addressing the issue of self-pity, acknowledge that it does provide a type of self-support through the "poor me" mind-set. In this activity, patients commiserate with themselves about their plight. At the same time emphasize the pitfalls of self-pity. For patients who have a tendency to slip into this maladaptive response, *self-pity rescue* may be needed (Sharoff, 2002, 2004).

SELF-ADVOCACY TRAINING

From the moment of symptom onset, chronic and terminal illness patients must face one of the gargantuan institutions in the world–the health care system. Patients must deal with doctors, nurses, and therapists who can be difficult, condescending, and dismissive for any number of reasons. Patients must deal with employers and coworkers who may not understand their plight. They must deal with spouses and children who are frustrated and incensed by changes in the patient. In other words, patients, in a highly vulnerable state in the crisis phase of their illness, suddenly find themselves facing a hostile, uncaring, and impersonal world.

An advocate is needed at this point. In the beginning, the advocate is often someone external to the medically unsavvy, beleaguered patient, who champions his/her cause. The advocate may be a relative, spouse, adult child, neighbor, clergyman, fellow parishioner, someone from the human resources department, or a visiting nurse. He/she becomes part of the treatment team and serves as an intermediary for the patient. For instance, the advocate may go to doctor appointments with the patient and present the needs of the patient. The advocate may talk to supervisors, coworkers, spouse, or family members, voicing the need for patience and continued support. If no adequate advocate can be found, then someone will have to be trained or groomed to fulfill this role. A spouse or adult child would be ideal for this role, but they may be too overcome with hostility toward the patient, which would prevent them from being an adequate advocate. However, as the disease continues, patients will need to become their own champion through *self-advocacy training*. By developing this capacity, they will not only strengthen themselves and build self-esteem, but also decrease their dependency on others. Here are the roles of the advocate:

1) She or he presents the patient's side of things, and offers a perspective to others so they can understand why the patient needs certain things or cannot do certain things. This is the *role of defender*.
2) She or he justifies the inability to fulfill role demands and expectations. This justification is not just for others but also for oneself, when the patient becomes self-demeaning and self-critical. The

intention is to vindicate the patient of blame, by advancing arguments that clear away accusations. This is a *vindicator or justifier role*. The vindicator role is not an apologist role. The patient needs to stay clear of having to apologize to others for having an illness, for being disabled, or for dying.

3)   She or he makes recommendations for how others can help the patient. This is an *educator* role. It helps others to understand the illness and its consequences.

4)   She or he acts as a *protector*. This involves setting limits on others when they are intrusive, condescending, demeaning, or hostile. This role can turn the patient into his own champion.

Self-advocacy often requires *assertiveness training* to speak up for one-self and not back down when others are pressuring for a different outcome. Patients may need to be trained in refusal assertiveness (e.g., declining the role of chauffeur when feeling too much pain) and request assertiveness (e.g., asking for help when fatigued) (Kelly, 1982). The latter is presented to people pleasers who have an irrational need for approval. *Entitlement training* can supplement assertiveness training, along with a discussion about patient rights (Alberti and Emmons, 1978).

Some patients feel guilty about fighting for their own rights when others are being deprived of what they need. Self-instruction training can help expunge guilt. Here is an example of self-talk for this purpose.

Guilt-Expunging Self-Talk

I am not bad because I became ill. I have nothing to apologize for.

I will not blame myself because I've become disabled, or a dying person, or a chronic pain patient.

Being ill is not bad and I am not bad when I disappoint others.

It is unfortunate if I disappoint others. It is not awful and I am not awful.

I do not want to disappoint others, but many times that happens when someone has an illness.

EXONERATION TRAINING

Besides self-instruction training, CCT has developed an alternative method to expunge guilt—*exoneration training*. This coping skill frees patients from the charge of irresponsibility and allows them to feel blameless and innocent when role responsibilities are not carried out. This skill is an important vehicle for supporting self-esteem and a positive self-concept. It works to dismiss entrenched, habitual, overlearned thinking leading to guilt and shame. It is a *self-installed response* that challenges and protests hypercritical thinking. It utilizes rational, realistic thinking but also makes use of paradoxical and behavioral techniques. The skill is developed in a legalistic, judicial format that is repeated over and over until guilt and shame are expunged.

The **first step** is *determining what is the nature of the crime*, or what the patient feels guilty about. For example, some medical patients feel ashamed of their appearance as a result of their disease, treatment, or treatment side effects. Behind their hatred of how they look and nonacceptance of self is self-condemnation for becoming "ugly" and not meeting appearance standards. There are other patients who feel ashamed because they have gained or lost weight, changed skin color, lost hair, became bloated, or lost a part of their body (e.g., a breast or a leg) as a result of surgery. There are other patients who charge themselves with selfishness for disappointing others by not fulfilling role duties (e.g., as a sex partner, housewife, or chauffeur for the children) or abandoning a role (e.g., jobholder).

The **second step** is *placing the patient on trial* for this charge *and charging him/her with a crime* ("I am guilty of gaining weight while taking prednisone. My crime is becoming unattractive, because being overweight is not allowed."). During the trial, the patient is placed in his/ her customary position of being an angry, hypercritical persecutor of self. Taking the role of prosecuting attorney, the patient presents the charges to an imaginary jury within the self. The irrational and unrealistic causes for the supposed crime need to be aired without reservation and with full condemnation ("I have not overcome my fatigue or carried out my required responsibilities to my family," "I should not have gotten breast cancer and lost my breast."). The therapist can join the prosecution team by acting as the patient's alter ego (therapist as patient: "There is no excuse for getting bloated and turning yellow, just because I have viral hepatitis."). The therapist encourages the patient to continue engaging in self-criticism and self-condemnation. This has a paradoxical benefit, to prescribe irrational thinking in the hope of stirring defiance against this harsh, mean-spirited way of treating oneself.

At this point some patients' intellect may "click on" and admit that the charges against themselves are absurd and further criticism is unwarranted or excessive. Finally growing tired of being self-critical, they come to the emotional realization that self-hatred and self-condemnation are ridiculous.

However, there are others who continue to feel guilty and ashamed and they move on to **step three.** At this point *the intellect is summoned to present a rational, reasonable defense of self.* The intellect counters irrational, unrealistic thinking ("Why am I guilty for having a body that changes against my desires?"). In the therapy session, the patient first airs the logical argument for the defense openly, with the aid of the therapist who acts as the patient's alter ego. Then the patient presents the defense internally, with the therapist observing the covert process. This is followed up in homework sessions where the same dialogue occurs between the internal prosecuting and defense attorneys. The intent is partly to help the patient broaden his/her thinking and impartially hear an objective, logical argument. It continues the ideas from cognitive restructuring to chip away at entrenched thinking. At this point many dismiss the charges against themselves, because the evidence has been refuted by the defense team of patient and therapist.

If guilt is still felt, patients move on to **step four.** That occurs when steps one to three have failed to change irrational, automatic thinking. In step four the *patient becomes the jury and decides the guilt or innocence of the accused.* At this point, some patients will intellectually rule themselves "not guilty" of their supposed crime, because logic and objectivity have swayed them. Yet, on an emotional level, they continue to feel guilty. If that is the case, patients are asked to repeat the first four steps of the exercise each day until negative emotions have been expunged. A daily time is arranged for practicing this exercise. Exoneration training then becomes a daily ritual or ordeal.

Highly entrenched, irrational thinkers, though, will still find themselves guilty as charged and still carry a residue of shame. They are not able to alter deep level feelings, even though intellectually they concede that their thinking is unreasonable. In that case, CCT wants these patients to face their thinking and take responsibility for it. In **step five,** *patients are asked to admit their supposed "crime" to themselves and others.* Examples include:

- I am guilty of putting myself first and allowing my fatigue and muscle weakness to keep me from completing my chores.
- I am guilty of becoming ugly and that is not allowed.
- I am guilty of developing a terminal disease and leaving my family to fend for themselves.

Step six has the patient act as a judge and *issue a sentence for committing the crime.* The patient qua judge may hesitate in ordering a punishment, but the therapist should encourage that one be given. An actual punishment is then exacted, such as no dinner one night a week, cleaning the house when feeling tired, or sleeping on the floor one night a week. In part, the punishment, while usually silly, acts as an ordeal (Haley, 1984) for thinking irrationally. There is a paradoxical reason for doing this, to arouse indignation in the patient for being punished for an unjustly charged offense. If the patient defies the therapist—which is what is wanted—s/he surrenders self-castigation. At the same time the exercise grants release from self-castigation for the supposed misdeed.

Finally, the patient measures how much guilt or shame is still present after sentencing and takes his/her punishment. If guilt is still at a moderate level or higher, then the entire exercise is repeated the following day along with the punishment.

From a behavioral standpoint, the exercise has several benefits. First, it stops the daily, obsessive castigation of self and relegates it to a specific time of day, as in the case of worry management (Barkovec et al., 1983; Sharoff, 2002). This puts the activity of self-condemnation under stimulus control, to only happen at a particular time instead of randomly. Second, a response substitution technique is used by allowing the intellect to defend the self and counter irrational thinking and negative emotion. The use of punishment makes irrational thinking costly. Negative reinforcement then acts to discourage beliefs leading to guilt. (See disc for patient worksheet.)

SUMMARY

Having a chronic or terminal illness requires substantial support. Being able to provide that support to oneself is most desirable. One self-support skill is self-boosting, where patients focus on what they are doing well and minimize what is not done well. Self-compassion is promoted, which includes permission giving, mercy, and soft-heartedness. Self-advocacy is important, where patients work to educate, protect, defend, and justify their behavior to others. If there is significant guilt due to not meeting others' expectations, then the skill of exoneration can be used to expunge it.

Part III

Coping Skills
for Alienation Phase

Chapter 8

Uncertainty Tolerance

There is so much that is uncertain in my life. My wife wants a bigger house, which I can afford, and we are cramped in our present home. But I hesitate to take on a bigger mortgage. If I die, then she is stuck with larger payments. I don't know what to tell her.

—Jack, cancer survivor

My chest feels as if it is being choked, like an elephant is sitting on it. I feel terribly scared when this happens and I worry, 'Is this the big one? Should I call 911 again?' They're sick of hearing from me. What do I make of myself?

—Bruce, angina patient

"What's next?" medical patients ask. "When will my symptoms cease? Will my disease return? Will the side effects of treatment end at some point? Will I have to give up work and go on disability? Will I be able to support my family and keep my house?"

Terminal illness patients have other pressing questions. They not only wonder about their disease but about such overwhelming matters as, "When will I die? How much will I suffer before I die? Is there an afterlife? What will happen to my loved ones, my possessions, and my life's work once I am gone?"

While chronic and terminal illness patients' bodies change for the worse, they, like anyone else, want to prepare for their future while not knowing what lies ahead. At the same time, health providers, in so many cases, cannot provide any clear-cut answers. While everyone faces uncertainty in their lives, medical patients have little they can count on. They cannot be sure their bodies, employers, health providers, or significant others will come through for them. Each direction they think of taking offers no guarantee. They find themselves swimming in a vast sea of uncertainty that is both maddening and enervating. Part of the reason disease is so unpleasant is because it creates secondary conditions like uncertainty, which in turn creates a derivative condition, anxiety. Yet, uncertainty cannot be eradicated and because of that, patients need to possess the vital skill of *uncertainty tolerance*. Without it, peace of mind will be minimal. This chapter focuses on how to relate to uncertainty and reduce its disturbing effects.

CRISIS PHASE TREATMENT OF UNCERTAINTY

When symptoms first arise or when the diagnosis is initially given, uncertainty quickly turns to anxiety. While uncertainty cannot be remedied, anxiety can be reduced to a livable level. Helping patients remain calm in the crisis phase is a primary treatment task. This section offers a basic anxiety reduction program for that purpose.

ANXIETY REDUCTION TRAINING

To increase willingness to practice these skills, patients need to understand the physiology of anxiety. Anxiety on a physical level is a matter of sympathetic arousal, where heart rate, pulse, breathing, adrenaline, blood sugar, and muscular tension increase. Because the body speeds up, the antidote is to slow it down.

To know when to quiet autonomic arousal, *self-monitoring* is imperative; it informs patients about when to inaugurate the other skills discussed in this section. To diminish anxiety when it is too intense, patients have to stay aware of their internal state. Self-monitoring also clarifies what the many physiological sensations in the body actually mean, regarding what to ignore, what has to be lived with, and what to become alarmed about.

For example, Bruce experienced many changes in his body after his heart attack. He would become frightened when he experienced various pains and twinges that he never had before. Self-monitoring his body on an hourly basis (see form below), he began to know how his damaged heart operated. He was able to distinguish between uncomfortable but routine sensations, referred to as stable or classical angina, and unstable angina, a sign of more serious heart trouble. Self-monitoring told him what types of activity would bring on angina attacks. Once he knew what to be concerned about and what to ignore, he felt far less anxious, and this in itself lessened his angina.

A simple time-interval self-monitoring form breaks down the hours of the day. Every hour the patient writes in the highest level of a negative emotion experienced in that time period (1 = mild; 2 = moderate; 3 = moderate to severe; 4 = severe; 5 = extreme level). The key number is three, when anxiety or a physical sensation is at a moderate to severe level. When at that level or higher, tactics to lower autonomic arousal should certainly be implemented. See disc for form.***

Once aware that anxiety and autonomic arousal are too high, then *relaxation* exercises ought to be employed. Types of exercises include deep breathing, progressive muscle relaxation (Jacobson, 1938), autogenic training (Schultz and Luthe, 1969), or guided imagery (Shielkh, 1983; Lang, 1977). See disc for handout regarding these skills. If anxiety in general is too intense, meditation can be employed on a daily basis to bring about an overall lowering of tension (Benson, 1975). While finding a comfortable, distraction-free setting is most desirable for practicing these techniques, that is not possible in many cases. Hence, medical patients will also need to be shown techniques to relax in the midst of tension-provoking situations (e.g., talking to a doctor, taking a medical test, taking injections). See Coping Skills Manual for examples (2004).*** For homework, patients practice cognitive rehearsal. Have them identify situations where they have become tense and then imagine being in the same scene, becoming calm and peaceful by using a stress reduction exercise. The goal throughout is anxiety amelioration, not anxiety removal.

To coordinate when to do what when feeling anxious, *self-instruction training* is practiced. In addition to cueing relaxation tactics, it orients the individual about what to think, how to act, and how to manage emotions (Meichenbaum, 1977; Meichenbaum and Jaremko, 1983). A self-dialogue is developed when preparing for an anxiety-provoking situation, facing the situation, becoming aroused, and afterward. Cognitive rehearsal is then employed, where patients imagine dealing with the situation successfully using a self-dialogue. The homework involves exposure to anxiety-provoking situations using that self-dialogue.

To increase the ability to relax in anxiety-provoking situations, *systematic desensitization* can be employed (Wolpe, 1973). This is a covert conditioning procedure where patients categorize events and actions that cause anxiety in ascending order. Each activity is imagined and a relaxation technique is used when anxiety occurs.

If patients continue to worry about health-related matters, then *worry management training* can be employed (Barkovec et al., 1983; Sharoff, 2002). The patient is told only to worry at a specific time (a stimulus control tactic), which becomes the "appointment" to worry. If the patient worries at other times, then ***thought stopping*** (Wolpe, 1958) or any sensory diversion technique (Sharoff, 2002) can have the same effect. For instance, when anxious, the individual can imagine the opening episode of a favorite television show or one's bedroom as a child but in minute detail to help clear the mind. While having the worry session, the patient imagines the situation becoming worse (Craske et al., 1992). This will aid ***habituation*** where the patient mentally becomes accustomed to a worse-case scenario. For some diseases, patients can use ***time projection***, where they fast-forward six months to a year ahead when they have grown used to living with the disease and have made strides in solving any difficulties (Lazarus, 1968). See disc for evaluation form to assess progress.***

ANXIETY ACCOMMODATION TRAINING

There is also an indirect way to lower anxiety, by accommodating to the emotion. This will address the secondary problem of being anxious about being anxious. This is a problem where disease causes intense anxiety, which in turn causes anxiety about having the unpleasant feeling of anxiety. Hating to feel that way, a demand is made to eliminate the stressful life. When anxiety continues unabated, a feeling of being out of control ensues, which only causes more anxiety. A vicious circle thus ensues.

While medical patients dislike being anxious, their life, realistically, will be beset with worry. A disease is threatening their existence, lifestyle, or financial stability and that is frightening. Being anxious makes sense. Logically, people should worry and feel dread to some degree when their body is diseased. People do not just *feel* out of control, they literally *are* out of control. They will be unable to cease feeling anxious because of the real-life dangers they face.

How can this problem be treated? The answer is ***anxiety accommodation***. In presenting this cognitive skill to patients, we emphasize the following points:

a)   Accept the fact that with so much changing and so little known about what will happen next, you will experience far more uncertainty and anxiety in your life than you experienced previously.

b)   Your life will feel more uncomfortable, because apprehension is discomforting, and that cannot be avoided.

c)   At various times anxiety will appear suddenly and become intense, and that comes with the territory of being threatened by disease or the treatment for it. Accept the fact that at various times you will feel highly uncomfortable when anxiety peaks. It will pass.

d) Stress reduction tactics can reduce anxiety but not remove it entirely. This means you must become accustomed to feeling uneasy, threatened, apprehensive, and insecure, especially in the crisis phase when so little is known about the disease, and coping skills have not been well developed.

e) Once you come to terms with this fact and accept being anxious, you will be better able to coexist with apprehension as an undesirable, daily condition. You will feel less concerned when it appears.

A self-instruction training dialogue can be employed that incorporates all these ideas.

As medical patients learn how to reduce their anxiety and accommodate to feeling apprehensive, they will be better able to manage the feeling of crisis and cope with instability. When that occurs they are able to move into the post-crisis phase. To progress further, though, to feel more consolidated, they will need to know in general how to address uncertainty in their life.

THREAT MANAGEMENT TRAINING

Uncertainty is far more of a problem when there is the possibility of danger, to oneself or loved ones. A skill is needed to respond to threat appropriately, and that is *threat management.*

Medical patients face many threats because they are often caught in an avoidance-avoidance conflict and are uncertain of which negative situation will harm them the least or the most. For instance, choosing to shun treatment or be treated but live with debilitating side effects. With either choice there is a threat to well-being, and that is what makes uncertainty so difficult to live with.

Threat management will help medical patients form a correct response to threat. It allows people to adequately face danger and coexist with it. With this ability, uncertainty will still cause anxiety, but it can be kept at a manageable level. Threat management includes three subskills: a) risk determination, b) risk readiness positioning, and c) activation management (Sharoff, 2002).

RISK DETERMINATION

Risk determination is the ability to identify degrees of risk. Threats are measured regarding their danger to the individual. It is performed in three steps.

    1)   Determine if an event could have potential to cause harm. The fear is changed to a hypothesis so it is not taken for granted as a definite danger. Next, the hypothesis is tested by collecting data for the purpose of accurately characterizing the situation as dangerous or not dangerous. If the data indicates that there is a legitimate threat, then a third step is performed: estimating when the danger will actually become a menace to well-being.

    2)   Estimate the severity of a threat. This is an ability to determine how much of a problem a threat can cause, or how grave is the danger to the person. It measures a threat. For instance: how severe do the side effects have to be before a medication is terminated? What is the likelihood that surgery may not work or cause more problems?

    3)   Estimate risk susceptibility. This is an ability to determine how much the individual is vulnerable to a threat, because of either internal or external variables. It estimates how much risk a danger poses. For instance: how much is a marriage susceptible to breaking apart because the patient is not able to perform role duties?

Risk determination allows patients to use their intellect to assess threats instead of their unconscious mind, which is so often influenced by irrational, unrealistic fears. The unconscious mind identifies threats long before the conscious mind realizes that there is a danger ahead. However, the fears of the unconscious mind are often excessive and unwarranted. Situations are characterized as dangerous when that is often not the case. Consequently, the conscious mind, using the intellect, needs to scientifically assess danger. See disc for evaluation form to assess progress in developing risk determination.***

RISK READINESS POSITIONING

Once a risk determination is made, a response to the threat has to be formulated, and that involves the skill of risk readiness positioning. *The risk readiness position (RRP) is an organized, deliberate, internal response that coordinates effective management, physiology, and behavioral intention.* It formulates the appropriate degree of response to a situation. The RRP is not a response to the stimulus but a response to the risk determination conclusion. It is a response to the belief about the degree of risk present in the situation. In general, the RRP has to accurately correspond to or match the level of challenge or danger that is present at that moment. While the RRP should mostly reflect present factors, potential future events will also be considered. There are three risk readiness positions.

1. Inert State

The lowest level of response is called an *inert state*. This RRP is adopted in the following circumstances. There is danger facing the individual but at most it is only mild. The danger is too distant to immediately harm the person. The danger is uncertain, indefinite, or amorphous; there are not enough facts now to characterize the situation as danger-ous. There are difficulties impinging on the individual (e.g., symptoms, treatment side effects), but they are being managed.

In the inert state, the mind and body are supposed to be calm and at rest. Effort is made to minimize concerns, to have little on the mind. If uncertainty becomes vexing about some danger, **proximal thinking** and **no-mind-no-thing** are promoted to stay in the here and now. To facilitate that, **sensory diversion** training and **thought stopping** are used. The intent is not to concentrate on any threat, but to focus on other life matters, and enjoy them as much as possible. Self-conflict about what to do next is halted using **worry management**. Problem solving about what to do next is suspended. The goal is creating a state of inner peace.

2. Alert Phase

The next higher level of activation is an *alert phase*. This RRP is adopted in the following cases. One, there is at least a moderate threat to well-being or challenge to oneself that needs to be watched. Two, there is a severe threat to well-being that has to be confronted at some time but not immediately. In that case only *moderate guardedness* is necessary. On a physical level, the body should be relaxed and autonomic arousal is kept at a minimal level. On a cognitive level, the patient: a) gathers information about the threat, b) monitors if the danger is becoming more menacing, c) forms contingency plans, d) reviews plans and offers changes to them, e) problem-solves about what to do should the danger escalate, f) reviews skill development to assess if they are adequate to cope with the danger, and g) if skills appear to be lacking, effort is expended on developing abilities. In part, the alert phase prepares someone for active mobilization. During this time a patient may make changes in his/her lifestyle to avoid future deterioration, physically or financially. For instance, there may be a change in role duties and role allocation within the family.

3. Active Mobilization

The third and highest RRP is active mobilization on both a mental and physical level. This RRP is adopted in the following circumstances. There is a severe *and* immediate danger to self. Contingency plans developed in the alert phase need to be executed. Physically, responding with a higher level of autonomic arousal is appropriate. Cognitively, the mind is engaged in combating the challenge to well-being. There is total concentration on the threat at hand. Skills are deployed. Further problem solving is occurring.

For example, a terminally ill patient with little time to live should be operating in an active mobilization state. Activities for this RRP would be saying goodbye to loved ones, reviewing the will, giving away possessions, and finalizing funeral arrangements. However, until the terminally ill patient knows that his death is imminent, a more appropriate risk readiness position would be an alert state, where the disease is monitored and planning occurs about what to do *if* the disease progresses. In this alert phase, more of the activity is occurring on a psychological level, where the patient may perform a life review, identify emotions, deal with them, and stay alert to new feelings as they emerge. At the same time, effort is made to keep the body as calm as possible.

ACTIVATION MANAGEMENT

The third component of threat management is activation management. This involves *ongoing work with the mind and body to adjust the RRP up or down.* Activation management is a dynamic, continuing process of adjusting the RRP to correspond to the level of perceived threat, then or in the future. It works to monitor autonomic arousal. If the RRP is too high, then anxiety-reduction techniques are employed to lower autonomic arousal. If the RRP is too low, then the patient has not adequately assessed risk. Risk determination is then used to accurately estimate danger.

One of the major tasks of activation management is curtailing unfettered rumination—reactive, emotionally driven processing of events—while commissioning a *deliberate, dispassionate response to danger.* Hence, an inhibitory skill is required using self-instructions ("Calm down. Quell emotions. Pull back. Become objective. Think about the situation."). Then, the process moves on to other skills such as *objectivity, problem-solving, hypothesis testing,* and *relaxation.*

THREAT MANAGEMENT ERRORS

Medical patients often commit one of several errors when dealing with perceived threats to themselves. Each of the errors below increase anxiety and cause uncertainty to be more of a problem. The following discussion will provide guidelines for health providers about how their patients should respond to threats to well-being.

1) *A premature determination is made that there exists a threat to well being.*
   Once there is concern about a health issue, data needs to be collected to determine if a supposed problem is legitimate danger to the patient. Many medical patients err by making only a superficial investigation of the facts before becoming frightened. They rush to judgment based on meager evidence. They feel the situation is more dangerous than it actually is.
   For example, Richard was a single man living independently in his own home. During the last few weeks, his MS became progressively worse. While he continued to work regularly and remained self-supporting, his physical deterioration stimulated fear that he would soon be forced to leave his job and go on disability. Without knowing if this would be necessary, he imaged a string of situations that frightened him even more. He predicted that on disability he would not be able to pay his bills and would then be forced to ask his parents for money to keep his home, something he hated to do. He eventually believed that he would have to live with his parents, and surrender his autonomy. Once he moved in with them, he assumed that they would control him totally.
   Fearing great risk to his lifestyle and independence, he adopted an RRP of active mobilization. Autonomic arousal was high as he readied his mind to face situations that had not yet materialized. He experienced the sadness of leaving his job and

coworkers, before he knew if that would be necessary. He felt the embarrassment of asking his family for money, before he even made the request. He executed contingency plans to protect himself (e.g., calling friends to ask if he could live with them after he sold his home) when they were unnecessary.

What should Richard have done instead? He needed to adopt a *periodic alert state*, where he would *collect data on his current condition but suspend judgments about where his life was heading*. Most of the time he should stay in an *inert state*, where he would remain in the here and now, not jump into the future, and wait to learn if his disease would progress or deteriorate. Then, with enough facts, he might assess if there was a definite trend. Activation management in the meantime would work to quiet his mind and body. Anxiety reduction techniques would be employed in this effort.

2) *A search for danger occurs even though risk determination cannot identify a definite threat.*

There are many types of diseases that leave patients highly uncertain about their future. There are diseases that fluctuate between improving and deteriorating but over the long term remain stable and allow patients to maintain their lifestyle. There are diseases that are stable but have a set of symptoms that appear alarming and unnerving. There are diseases that are stable and stay in remission but there is no guarantee that will continue.

Faced with uncertainty, some patients err by pushing to learn where their life is heading. They stay keenly tuned into the ebb and flow of their disease, to detect if their condition is worsening. They yearn to know what any symptom means. Every difference in body functioning is noted and studied carefully. Anxiety is rampant, as risk determination becomes a daily if not hourly part of life. Repeat visits to doctors or emergency rooms are common in an effort to know if a symptom portends future trouble. Uncertainty, for these patients, is debilitating.

Patients such as these have a risk readiness position that hovers between high alert and active mobilization. However, for diseases like the ones discussed, that RRP is incorrect. These patients are too watchful, too guarded, too responsive to bodily changes, and too engaged in planning. Instead, *an inert RRP is more appropriate for diseases that have an indeterminate, vague prognosis.* Patients with such a disease need to learn to live calmly and peacefully with a set of symptoms that offer no clear direction about the future.

A calm mental state and relaxed body is needed until there is a definite alteration in disease progression. When health threats are amorphous, the goal is coexisting peacefully with a condition that is difficult to figure out, takes many twists and turns, may cause physical distress, but does not place the patient in *immediate* danger one way or another. In this situation, risk determination should not be performed too frequently to avoid unnecessary anxiety.

3) *Threat contemplation continues until a definite answer is forthcoming.*
    Once a threat to well-being has been determined, patients then have to determine how soon they will be in danger. If the threat is imminent, then the RRP needs to be active mobilization. However, if the threat is not imminent, but danger to self is a definite possibility at some point, then the appropriate RRP should be an inert state most of the time with periods of alert to gauge the degree of danger present. In the meantime, threat contemplation should cease.

This would be appropriate in the following cases. One: there is a chronic, progressively deteriorating disease but the rate of deterioration is slow and gradual. Two: the course of deterioration is erratic but there is no clear indication of where the disease is heading. Three: there is eventual danger to oneself but the course of deterioration takes a long period of time. In each of these situations, patients need to know how to live with their disease in a calm manner. At times the patient may move into an alert phase to assess his condition but overall should remain inert.

To illustrate this point, we will return to the case of Richard. He knows that his condition is getting worse, but the deterioration has been gradual. He faces many psychological threats to his well-being, such as eventually changing his independent lifestyle and becoming dependent on others, but that may not occur for a long time. Yet, he cannot stop contemplating the dangers ahead in his life, even though they are not confronting him there and then.

So what should he do? One: formal risk determination will only need to occur periodically and with caution, and not based on day-to-day changes in health status. Two: his mind has to be trained to ignore daily perturbations of the disease. The definition of threat should only be given when a long-term trend is clear. Daily changes in his body are noted but no conclusions should be drawn about them. Three: effort must be made to restrain emotional responses to one day's poor functioning. Curtailing worry will be necessary, using such skills as *sensory diversion, no-mind-no-thing, thought stopping, psychological distancing, and relaxation.* Four: if a negative long-term trend in health status is noted, then Richard can arrange time for grieving, expression of emotion, and thinking about his problem. While the idea of making an appointment to emote sounds strange, that is preferable to his breaking down at work with intense emotions, dread, and worry. The overall goal is to avoid random grieving over daily changes in health status because that will only exhaust his psychological reserves, interfere with daily role functioning, and not necessarily lead to resolution of his emotional conflicts.

4) *The degree of activation is too high for the threat of the moment.*

While medical patients have a lot to worry about, many of them err by being overwrought and overemotional about their physical condition. They concentrate too much on health matters and not enough on other more pleasant matters that can be a diversion from the disease. Their degree of activation is often too high for the threat *of the moment.* To again use Richard as an example, the fact is he is still able to manage an independent life, and as long as that is the case he is not in immediate danger. His RRP needs to reflect that. Yes, he does need to make contingency plans, which is part of going on periodic alert status. But once problem solving has formulated a plan, further planning is not necessary. His mind should then move back to an inert status, tuned into daily pursuits and turned away from his health.

5) *The estimate of threat is too severe.*

Many medical patients err in their estimate about the real danger of a threat. Their thinking is unrealistic. For example, Richard imagines living with his parents as catastrophic. He remembers how they were when he was a child and hated being under their control. He assumes that they will be the same when he is a disabled adult, and that he is the same person that he was as a child. Of course, that is not the case. He has matured, acquired skills, and is far more capable of managing infringements. Likewise, his parents have also had a chance to mature. In essence, he overestimates the threat facing him and by doing so causes himself unnecessary anxiety. While living with his parents may not be as pleasant as his independent life, it probably will not be as bad as he pictures it. He also could find the benefits in this unwanted situation, if he would practice being a "*bright side thinker*" (discussed below).

6) *There is an excessive fear of susceptibility to threat.*

Many patients err in the belief that they will be far more affected by a given threat than they actually will be. They believe that risk cannot be controlled. Thinking this way, the outcome appears far more calamitous and the threat appears far more ominous. Yet, the facts do not support their assumptions. Or, the facts are correct, but the patient has better ability to manage the threat than she/he believes. Patients who commit this error lack self-assurance that they can respond adequately to a difficult situation.

Richard, for example, believes he will be far more susceptible to disease progression. When he has a few bad days, he quickly believes that he is on greased skids sliding headlong into a loss of self-management, even though his disease history reveals an erratic type of progression where he gets worse, improves, gets worse, etc.

We will now discuss two ways of thinking that can lessen the onerous effects of uncertainty. One is optimism training and the other is re-attribution training.

OPTIMISM TRAINING

An uncertain situation would not be so anxiety provoking if one knew that it would eventually turn out positively. While there is no way to assure that, people may assume desirable outcomes will occur, or expect that they can be attained. This is termed an optimistic outlook.

Optimism and its opposite, pessimism, are similar in that they both engage in illusory thinking. The mind believes something will happen based more on faith than fact. This is a form of self-deception that works in favor of the individual, whereby the future is not known but one presumes that it will be good or bad. Optimists assure themselves that the future will be positive, while pessimists assure themselves that the future will be bleak or depriving. By doing so, the former feels carefree, bright, and buoyant, while the latter feels gloomy, dour, and worried. Pessimism makes uncertain situations far scarier, because of the belief that the worst will happen.

Optimism is influenced by expectancy and values (Edwards, 1954), which in turn affects motivation. Because there is confidence that a valued goal can be achieved, there is more likelihood that a helpful action will be pursued. There is more willingness to combat adversity. Optimists are more assured and trust that a valued outcome can be achieved, even in the face of adversity. Hence, uncertainty will not bother them nearly as much as pessimists.

Being an optimist pays several dividends (see Carver and Scheier, 1999, for review of the literature). They are able to resist developing depression and anxiety. They are more satisfied with the disease treatment, have less presurgery distress, and are more resilient in the face of postsurgery distress. Evidence is emerging that optimists are better copers and have a coping advantage over pessimists. Optimists use active coping strategies such as securing information about the disease and engaging in planning for recovery, while pessimists use avoidant coping strategies such as denial, behavioral disengagement, escaping into sleep, and alcohol use. Optimists focus more on the positive aspects of their experience and find redeeming elements to otherwise negative situations. Optimists deal with substantial risks to well-being much better than pessimists.

Hope is a related variable to optimism and it too offers substantial benefits (see Snyder et al., 1999 for review of the literature). Higher hope is related to better coping, less dependency, less burnout, engagement in fewer behaviors that undermine recovery, better tolerance of pain, better body functioning in areas affected by disease, and better psychological adjustment to disease. High hope individuals find alternative pathways to a goal and have better compliance with the medical regimen. They find other pathways if their primary route to a goal is blocked. Overall, they think and feel more positively. Oppositely, low hope individuals feel more overwhelmed by their situations.

If a patient is an optimistic and hopeful person, then therapy only needs to underscore the importance of that outlook. The focus might shift to what could cause a change in that way of being or what could dampen hopefulness (e.g., the disease worsens, excessive bad news such as loss of a job).

If a patient is a pessimist, he/she is tempted to imagine the worst and then suffer worse consequences as a result. However, optimism and hopefulness can be trained. While optimism appears to be genetic, there is some evidence that pessimists can learn to become optimists (Shatte, 1999). Subjects have been trained to develop hopefulness. This can be accomplished by developing a capacity to become goal focused and motivated to work on pathways to reach the goal. Once patients realize that goals can be attained, this will raise their optimism and hope that the future can be beneficial. Uncertainty will not seem so overwhelming or dominate attention nearly as much.

A PROBLEM-SOLVING APPROACH

Here is a program for pessimistic, low hope individuals. It uses ideas from solutions-oriented therapy (de Shazer, 1985, 1988); self-management therapy (Rehm and Rokhe, 1988); and Snyder, Cheavens, et al. (1999).

1. Identify how the patient views his/her situation.
2. Characterize it as either an optimistic, pessimistic, or cautious position. A cautious position is a refusal to take a position about how situations will turn out, along with a preference to wait and see what will be faced before characterizing the situation.
3. Define what is an optimist, pessimist, or cautious person. Then have the patient declare which one s/he is. To measure optimism, providers can use the LOT-R scale (in Carver and Scheier, 1999) and to measure hope, providers can use the Adult State Hope Scale and the Adult Trait Hope Scale (in Snyder, Cheavens, et al., 1999).
4. Tell the patient about the benefits of being optimistic and hopeful, citing research outcome studies. The intention in doing this is to market the practice of optimism and create enthusiasm for being hopeful.
5. Identify the patient's goal state. It needs to be behaviorally specific and capable of being measured. Assess if the goal state is outside of the patient's area of influence.
6. Specify the ways to attain that goal. Use *area thinking* (Sharoff, 2002) to plot ways that patients can reach their goal, by finding actions within their area that can lead to goal attainment. Inquire how much they believe that these routes to attain the goal can be successful. Gain a measurement of their degree of confidence in their plan.
7. When engaging in area thinking, *problem-solving* will need to be utilized to select alternative ways to resolve a difficulty that is within a person's area of influence. To aid problem-solving, a *decision tree* can be used. It involves the following steps. Patients start out at a certain point: this may or may not happen. One possibility is selected (e.g., something will happen). The consequences from that possibility are plotted along with alternative

plans for dealing with each consequence. Likewise, the opposite possibility is selected (e.g., something will not happen). The consequences from that possibility are plotted as well, and alternative plans are made for that situation. Decision trees allow a person to see alternatives with action plans spread out before them, and that can ease uncertainty about what course to take.

8. Estimate how much of the goal state can be accomplished by those actions. This is a scaling question (Selekman, 1999): "If you could achieve 10 percent of your goal this week, what would you have to do?"

9. Explicate what the person would do if his/her primary path to achieving a goal were blocked. This is important because low hope people do not seek alternative paths when a primary path is blocked (Snyder, Cheavens, et al., 1999).

10. Use self-reinforcement to sustain working on the pathway to goal attainment. The reinforcer can be verbal praise ("Good job on getting up before 8 a.m.") or a tangible reward when the goal state is accomplished to varying degrees. This is a self-management strategy. Accompany this with self-affirmation statements such as, "I can make a difference in my life," "I can make myself happier despite the obstacles I face."

11. Specify what would sustain that person's motivation to continue working on attaining goals, and what would curtail that effort in the future? The intention is to identify causes for relapsing into pessimism and low hopefulness in advance, so there is a plan in place to manage problems as they emerge (Marlatt, 1985).

12. Secure an estimate (from 0 to 5, with five being highest motivation) of how motivated the patient is to work on this endeavor. Have the patient perform a motivation estimate daily to stay abreast of willingness to work on achieving the goal state.

13. When patients return to each session, inquire how much they have been able to attain the goal state between sessions and by how much (a scaling question). Discuss what was occurring and what skills were being used on those occasions that allowed them to be in the goal state. Finally, assign what is working to be continued into the future.

USE OF BRIGHT-SIDE THINKING

Another way to tolerate uncertainty is by becoming a person who does not have totally awful outcomes. That is, uncertainty would not be so frustrating if someone could see the good amidst the bad. Thinking this way assures a person of positive outcomes. It creates a tendency to perceive the beneficial aspects of an event. This can be called a "*positivity bias.*" Sharoff (2002) refers to it as **bright-side thinking.** Other expressions for this same activity include turning lemons into lemonade, seeing the glass as half-full, or turning gray skies blue.

Bright-side thinking is a cognitive-perceptual process where a person elects to overlook or sidestep negative factors and emotions that otherwise would be generated by an undesirable stimulus. Reflexively, the person mentally pulls back and scours the situation to find any redeeming aspects to it. Bright-side thinking transforms or reconfigures an error, mishap, unpleasant, troublesome occasion, or unfortunate occurrence into something that includes positive elements. It is a type of reframing where the same set of facts is viewed differently. In another regard, it creates a positive self-illusion regarding reality.

Bright-side thinking requires the subskill of *consequential thinking.* The person brainstorms (Osborn, 1963) to generate a list of possible consequences that may occur in a situation. From this list, positive outcomes are identified. Perception is then used to stay focused on them. This pushes the more obvious negative elements of the perceptual field into the background so they make less of an impact. Those negative elements can either be ignored or are dealt with at other times using *problem-solving.*

This thought pattern will have to be trained and sustained in patients who do not typically think that way. Below is a self-evaluation form that will help inculcate this ability.

Finding the Bright Side
1. What negative situations happened to me today? _____
2. What are the positive aspects of those situations? _____
3. What benefits can accrue to me as a consequence of those situations?
4. Did I stay focused on those benefits during the day? Y__ N __
5. How did I feel having done the above? _____

REATTRIBUTION TRAINING

As already noted, uncertainty is more of a problem to pessimists than optimists. Beliefs about causality sustain and influence pessimism and optimism. People tend to perceive causality in set ways, which is termed an *attribution style.* This section discusses how to change people's attribution, and how to think if someone wants to be an optimist.

Optimists will have a particular attribution style that differs from pessimists. A pessimistic attribution style will contribute to a feeling of helplessness and insecurity, while an optimistic style will forge a feeling of power, security, and control. Presuming one can influence the outcome state is termed self-efficacy (Bandura, 1997, 1982). The presence of self-efficacy leads to less anxiety about the future. Oppositely, if someone presumes that s/he has little ability to influence outcome, situations containing uncertainty will be harder to tolerate. They will lead to a feeling of helplessness, which in turn contributes to depression (Abramson et al., 1989).

Over time people will generalize that helplessness cannot be changed in other situations as well, even when there is actually more personal control (Seligman and Maier, 1967). This generalization has important implications for chronic and terminally ill patients. If a medical patient believes that she is helpless to change the course of her disease, she will also generalize that she is helpless in other contexts as well, such as the context of treatment. Thinking this way, she will be less willing to comply with the medical regimen. Her thinking will be, "Why put the effort in therapy if it will not produce results?" Thus, the more helpless medical patients feel, the more pessimistic they are. The more pessimistic they are, the less they will cope with their disease.

The perception of helplessness and the development of pessimism is shaped by beliefs about causality (the attribution). Those beliefs are stable over time and go across situations. People interpret events in a set way, which is termed an *explanatory style* (Abramson et al., 1978; Burns et al., 1989; Shatte et al., 1999). This is a predisposition to analyze events in a particular way, especially negative events like disease or inability to be helped or cured.

There are three dimensions of attribution that form the explanatory style (Shatte et al., 1999). One dimension deals with *internal-external attribution.* An internal attribution is a belief that the reason for a problem and the mainspring for a solution lie within the individual. For instance, the problem can be due to someone's emotional state, personality, or genetic makeup. An external attribution is a belief that the cause of a problem and the solution for it are mostly external to the individual. A second dimension deals with *stable versus changing forces.* This is an assumption that events are caused by enduring forces or short-lived, unstable forces. A third dimension deals with *global versus specific causes* for a situation. This is an assumption that events are caused by global or massive forces, or specific, narrow reasons. An example of the former is a general predisposition to be a certain way, or an overall structural failing in the individual. An example of the latter is a tendency to act a certain way only in a specific context.

As a generalization, "Pessimists tend to explain negative events in terms of internal, stable, and global causes, and attribute positive events to external, unstable, and specific causes. Conversely, optimists tend to explain negative events as due to external, unstable, and specific causes, while ascribing positive outcomes to internal, stable, and global attributes" (Shatte et al., 1999, p. 167). That is, pessimists think, "Bad events are due to forces within me (an internal attribution) that are significant. Those forces will stay the same (they are stable). Good things that happen to me I have little to do with (an external attribution), can change suddenly (an unstable situation), and are due to some narrow reason." Thinking this way, aversive events seem uncontrollable and beyond the individual, while positive events are not caused by the pessimist's good deeds and positive traits. Oppositely, optimists think, "I have a lot to do with making this good event happen (an internal attribution), and that good things will continue to happen to me (a stable situation). I have little to do with why bad things happen to me (an external attribution) but those bad things will not last long (an unstable situation) because they are due to some specific cause that will only have a short effect on the outcome of the situation." In time, pessimists develop an external-stable explanatory style ("Bad things that happen to me are beyond my control and will stay the same."). This explanatory style leads to a belief in personal low controllability—the feeling of helplessness.

Unless there is an effort to change, an individual's degree of pessimism stays constant across the lifespan (Burns and Seligman, 1989). Taking these conclusions into consideration, the hypothesis can be made that uncertainty will be less of a problem if a person could be converted to an optimistic attribution style. Specifically in regard to chronic or terminal illness, what would be an optimistic attribution style? "I am suffering because of external factors such as my disease and the side effects from treatment. However, that misery does not have to continue (it's unstable). The only reason I am miserable now is because my disease is acting up today. Tomorrow could be different (specific cause)."

What would be a pessimistic explanatory style? "I am suffering because if something rotten is going to happen it will happen to me, because something within me just invites disaster (an internal attribution). That's how it has always been with me (stable causation). I just don't have good luck. There's little I can do about that (due to massive reasons)."

Changing the above perspective would require an alteration in explanatory style. *Patients need to be trained to have an internal, stable, global attribution.* That would involve the following position that will need to be developed in patients: "I can make a difference in my situation (an internal attribution), because I can count on my abilities (a belief that a stable situation exists). I have coping skills that can be utilized in any situation like the present one (global use)." This explanatory style will raise self-confidence and forge self-efficacy. The future will not appear as scary, and uncertain situations will not be foreboding and ominous.

One way to develop an optimistic attribution style is by use of cognitive restructuring (CR). It will unmask self-fulfilling prophecies and pessimistic explanations that result in depletion of motivation and helplessness. It will treat unrealistic prophecies and "certainistic thinking" that maintains that suffering is definitely permanent and unalterable. CR would challenge this way of thinking by restructuring explanations that are not valid.

In using CR, patients will present situations where their explanatory style is identified. If incorrect, the attribution is challenged and replaced with the appropriate thought pattern. Over time, patients will become better able to recognize pessimistic and optimistic thinking. Two support activities are necessary: slowing down the rate of thinking and assuming an objective, nonemotional response.

An alternative way to develop an optimistic attribution style is by using a combination of coping skills. *Area thinking* will demarcate what can and cannot be changed by the individual and his/her support team (e.g., doctors, friends, nurses). Pathways are then identified for reaching the outcome state, using *problem-solving*. These two skills will help patients manage situations, which in turn can develop an internal attribution. It will increase faith in one's abilities (a stable self-image) and build self-assurance, which will develop a viewpoint that the self can make a difference across situations (global causation).

Summary

Uncertainty is a basic part of life for chronic and terminal illness patients. In the crisis phase it is mostly treated by use of anxiety reduction techniques such as self-monitoring, relaxation, and self-instruction training. Threat management will help with uncertainty by knowing how to deal with perceived threats. It consists of risk deliberation, risk readiness positioning, and activation management. There are three risk readiness positions: inert, alert, and active mobilization phases. Medical patients commit several errors in how they think, leading to the wrong risk readiness position. Two styles of thinking can ease uncertainty: optimism and an optimistic attribution style. Oppositely, pessimism leads to help-lessness, which in turn makes uncertainty harder to tolerate.

Bitterness Disposal Training

Sue, an interstitial cystitis patient, urgently wanted to be seen by a therapist because she had been feeling desperate about the pain caused by her disease. The therapist gladly agreed to show her a pain management technique, but her only response was an abrupt, "Next!" Somewhat surprised by her curt reply, he presented another way to psychologically manage discomfort. Halfway through, she again blurted out loudly, "NEXT." Startled by her anger, the therapist inquired what she found disagreeable about his ideas. "I have seen a lot of doctors and therapists," she said impatiently, "and no one understands my situation. I have severe pain. No one is taking that away. I cannot go on like this anymore. All you health providers have done one thing—let me down."

As disease lingers, chronic and terminally ill patients commonly experience what Sue feels—bitterness. This is a corrosive feeling that enervates the spirit and hardens the soul, leaving patients unprepared and unmotivated to live with their disease. Because of the massive effects of disease, some degree of bitterness can be expected. However, knowing how to dispose of bitterness is an important treatment task. This chapter will mostly address bitterness that arises from interpersonal situations. Chapter 10 will address how to treat bitterness directed toward the body. (The Coping Skills Manual discusses how to treat bitterness in resistant patients who refuse to change.)

THE BITTERNESS EXPERIENCE

What is bitterness? How is it experienced? It is a feeling of being anguished, tormented, and agitated. A mental pain exists that includes regret, sorrow, and indignation, because the embittered feel aggrieved about unjust and unworthy treatment they have had to suffer. They feel afflicted by wrongs and offenses that they believe have been committed against them. This causes them to harbor a "grudge" and appear caustic, as if they were carrying a chip on their shoulder. Deep resentment and a hostile, antagonistic stance pervades their interactions with others, resulting in impatience and inability to cope with life's routine frustrations.

Who is the object of bitterness? It can be a weak, infirm body, God, fate, or fortune that supposedly caused the illness, health providers who cannot deliver a cure, a demanding employer, insensitive coworkers, or loved ones. It can be institutions such as hospitals or insurance companies. Frequently, the bitterness is directed against others who have not wronged the patient, and in this regard it is displaced anger.

Another element of bitterness is disillusionment. It occurs when illusions about a person (the self or another individual) disintegrate and the reality about that person has to be faced. When that occurs, disenchantment is felt. At that moment, reality is a bitter truth. Reality may be the knowledge that a marriage will not survive, or cherished outcomes will not be realized. The task at that point is admitting the bitter truth to oneself and accepting its existence.

Some patients will not be aware of their bitterness, and providers need to make them aware that it is hidden behind other emotions. It can lurk behind depression, plaintive sadness, whining, self-pity, and fretful misery. It is characterized by disturbed sleep, changes in appetite, and problems concentrating. It can take the form of frequent irritation and exasperation with others.

We will now see how a coping skills model would treat two main causes of bitterness in medical patients. One is rejection from others and the second is frequent disappointment. For rejection, survival skills are listed. For disappointment, the skill of disappointment accommodation is presented. Another dominant cause of bitterness—deprivation—will be covered in chapter 12.

TREATMENT OF REJECTION

At the same time chronic and terminally ill patients struggle with their physical symptoms and treatment side effects, they are also forced to struggle with other people's negative responses to them because they are ill. Those responses are experienced as rejection.

There are several forms of rejection. It can range from total severing of a relationship (e.g., being dismissed from work, divorce) to partial rejection where another person withdraws from the relationship by decreasing communication and regular contact; a tie remains but it is tenuous. A more subtle form of rejection is "essence rejection." When this occurs, the medical patient's basic essence or goodness is dismissed, and she/he is only related to as a "poor soul." The patient is pigeonholed and stereotyped, reduced to being a diseased person first and foremost. A final form of rejection is projection. This occurs when medical patients reject themselves as having little worth. They then project this viewpoint onto others, assuming others think negatively of them.

REALITY DETECTION

In treating rejection, therapists face several problems. A patient may feel rejected when that is not the case. A patient fails to realize that she or he has been rejected. And finally, a patient is unsure of what the data indicates: is there rejection or not? In each case, the person needs help grasping reality. A skill is needed—*reality detection*—to learn what is actually occurring. This skill requires *descriptive judgment training*, to phenomenologically understand a situation as it is without preconception, evaluation, assumption, or interpretation. Patients are trained to follow a process without ascribing meaning, witnessing the flow of events, and describing them as they are with sensory-based judgments. After collecting a significant amount of data, patients ask themselves if there are enough facts present to judge meaning. If data is inconclusive, they are cautioned to suspend conclusions about meaning. If a patient feels confident to make a judgment about meaning, then she or he must question that proposition by asking, "How do I know that judgment is accurate? What is the supporting data?" To assess if the meaning is accurate, other meanings for the same data are proposed and the patient selects which meaning proposition best fits the data. In essence, reality detection trains patients how to perform cognitive restructuring within themselves.

ACCEPTANCE TRAINING

Once the patient determines that a rejection has occurred, then the next treatment task is accepting that fact. While sounding simple, acceptance is a most complicated activity. It involves four tasks: 1) emotional recognition of reality, 2) allowing reality into one's life, 3) coexisting with reality, and 4) accepting unwanted consequences.

1. Emotional Recognition of Reality

People can admit to something intellectually but emotionally refuse to recognize what is happening. This can occur in several ways. One can ignore the facts so they are not felt. The facts may be seen only fleetingly so they do not make much of an impression. The facts are "played down" or minimized. Rationalizations are offered to reduce the impact of intellectual knowledge. Each of these tactics circumvents and eludes the truth.

To address this problem, treatment needs to help patients emotionally recognize reality. An obvious approach utilizes confrontation, where reality is boldly presented to the patient to see the situation as it is. *Process comments* are used afterward to assess if the patient allowed the confrontation to make an impact ("What did you just do when you heard the facts I presented?"). If the facts make little impact, then the therapist makes another process comment, "How did you keep yourself from being affected by what I had to say?" Another option uses the Gestalt approach of experiencing the experience (Van de Reit et al., 1980). In this technique, the facts are held in view long enough to allow them to make an impression (Therapist: "Stop and look at what is. Notice how these facts affect you.").

The patient is then asked to grow accustomed emotionally to the facts as part of recognizing them. Recognition, in part, means not turning away from a fact because it is upsetting. Using the behavioral technique of habituation (Barlow, 1988), patients are asked to imagine the consequences of rejection as they are played out (e.g., seeing oneself unemployed, seeing oneself alone after a separation). They are then asked to imagine that same scene several times a day to gain repeated exposure to the feared and unpleasant facts, so they make less of a negative impact over time. Time projection (Lazarus, 1968) can also be used where the patient projects six months to a year after the rejection and sees how his/her life may be going at that time.

2. Allowing Reality into One's Life

Once there is a full recognition of reality, the next acceptance task is allowing that disliked reality into one's life. At this point some patients show confusion about acceptance, equating it with surrender or approval of something that is unwanted. Therapists need to differentiate between each of them, stipulating that they are free to combat reality and try to change it behaviorally (using a nonsurrender tactic), or disapprove of reality, which is an evaluative matter. However, at the same time, the patient must nevertheless face the facts at that moment in time.

When the facts are allowed into a patients' life, there will be an emotional reaction, e.g., sadness, anger. Traditional ego-supportive therapy techniques are most able to address those subsequent feelings, by allowing expression of feeling, acknowledging patient feelings, and validating them as something anyone might have in those circumstances. A therapist's warmth, caring, and compassion is needed at this point. Cognitive restructuring may be useless at this time if there is no irrational thinking about the rejection. The simple fact is that rejection hurts and it needs to be felt.

3. Coexisting with Reality

Once reality is admitted into a person's life, the next step is coexisting with a painful, unwanted situation. This involves the skill of *rejection tolerance.* Cognitive restructuring (CR) can be helpful to develop this ability. It will examine irrational, unrealistic thinking that paints an incorrect picture of personal capacity and what life will be like following the rejection. For example, the patient may predict, "I cannot live without him. I cannot be happy without him." CR can show the patient that her beliefs are incorrect, that living with the rejection is not awful and will not be awful, just unpleasant.

If patients have a hard time surrendering their irrational, unrealistic thinking, *imagery* can be used to reveal the consequences of doing so. For instance, the patient can be assigned a fantasy, where he thinks the irrational thought and then imagines a dark, rainy cloud following him during the week, drenching him, and making him miserable. The cloud stands for the negative consequences of subscribing to irrational beliefs.

If patients are having a difficult time dealing with the pain of rejection, then the focus needs to shift to *pain management training.* Self-instruction training is helpful for developing a capacity to tolerate a psychologically painful circumstance. For example: "I don't like what is happening to my life, but I am tough enough to handle it. I have dealt with other difficult matters and have coped with them. I am strong even though I don't feel that way now. Bear up. Withstand the pain. Show how tough I am. It will get better if I choose to move on. This won't crush me." To show the benefits of this approach, patients can engage in a ritual of thinking irrational, unrealistic beliefs on odd days of the week and the above self-dialogue on even days of the week and then note the difference.

To facilitate coexistence with reality, the problem of disapproving of reality and decrying what has happened will also have to be addressed. The negative consequences from doing so need to be listed, and patients are asked to take responsibility for them. In essence, the nonutilitarian aspect of focusing on the rejection has to be recognized.

4. Accepting Unwanted Consequences

The major unwanted consequence of rejection is pain, especially when someone does not want to be rejected. Patients need to be given a choice: reject the pain of rejection and hate it (which will keep the pain in the foreground), or focus on how to tolerate and cope with the pain (which will lessen it in the long run). The intention is to again force patients to take responsibility for bringing about their own negative emotions.

If patients choose to stay focused on their rejection, CCT would recommend that they learn pain management techniques, because their pain will increase if they stay focused on negative circumstances. If patients choose to tolerate the unwanted consequences, then the focus shifts to accepting those consequences.

Imagery and symbolic gesturing can be used to facilitate acceptance. For instance, a patient can imagine a cold, strong wind blowing against her (the symbol for rejection). At the same time she momentarily stops inhaling and brings her hands forward, feeling the muscles strain to keep the wind away. Then, she lowers her hands slowly and imagines letting the wind in, while at the same time she inhales (symbolizing letting the rejection into her life). Her hands relax as she does this. She imagines feeling the cold wind but sees herself bearing up against the cold. The technique is aimed at facilitating acceptance of an unwanted situation.

IDENTITY SCRUTINY

Rejection has a dramatic effect on identity. Melanie, for instance, suffered from chronic fatigue. It prevented her from being the action-oriented companion her husband desired in a wife. Over time he did more and more activities without her, while refusing to join her in activities she could participate in, which were mostly sedentary in nature.

When she could not do what he wanted, he would sigh, groan, shake his head, and roll his eyes. His anger and disenchantment with her were obvious. This nonverbal behavior gave Melanie a negative image of herself as an inadequate wife.

Melanie is faced with an important task when she feels rejected: *scrutinizing identity* that has been adversely affected by the rejection experience. This skill provides two main benefits. One: it identifies how someone is being portrayed, which in turn influences self-image and self-esteem. Two: it determines if that image is a true or accurate representation of self. That is, does the image not fit, fit in general, or only in specific situations?

Identity scrutiny is crucial to avoid sullying identity. Because rejection inevitably conveys the conceptualization of a person, there is a need to *forestall incorporating it into identity before examining it carefully.* Quite commonly, chronic or terminally ill patients are portrayed as deficient or damaged goods, and less worthy than others. If identity scrutiny does not become a routine activity following interactions, medical patients risk unconsciously acquiring a pejorative view of self.

Therapists must take patients through several steps when performing this skill. First, patients must restrain their emotional reaction to rejection, such as defensiveness or dejection. Second, patients need to assume an objective stance, which is necessary to view the situation dispassionately and intellectually. The intellect then reviews the images being conveyed. Next, other people's words or actions (that are taken as rejection) are described and the meaning put upon them is identified. This tells what the patient thinks his/her image is in other people's eyes. Finally, the patient decides if this image is accurate. If it is not accurate, then assess what makes it inaccurate.

If the portrayal of self is inaccurate, then it will need to be disposed of so it does not infect identity. One possibility is a direct refusal to accept the negative image ("This view of me is not accurate and I reject it."). Imagery can also be used. For instance, a trash can may be imagined where all the inaccurate conceptualizations are wrapped in paper and thrown away.

The next task is to *self-monitor* if the inaccurate image has infiltrated identity. How much does the patient feel diminished by the negative view of self, from zero to five? If there is a rating of three or more (indicating at least a moderate feeling of diminishment), then diminution training (see below) will need to be practiced.

If the negative image of the patient is accurate, then she/he will have to decide what needs to be done about that. Does the patient want to change some action to receive a more positive image? Can the patient change that behavior, given her medical condition? In the case of Melanie, she is not able to change her behavior, due to symptoms of her disease. Consequently, she must learn to adjust to receiving negative images of self. The skill of *imperviousness training* will help with this (see Chapter 12). It will allow patients to avoid being infected by other's negative images.

If the patient chooses to change a troublesome behavior of another person, then interpersonal skills are required, such as *communication ability, negotiation,* or *conflict resolution.* In the end, though, the patient may need to live with disappointing another person. At this point, helping him/her deal with guilt, shame, or embarrassment may be necessary, by learning the skill of exoneration training (see Chapter 7).

DIMINUTION TRAINING

When a rejection occurs, the negative image of self can become dominant and eclipse other self-images. The need at that time is to utilize *diminution training* to minimize the harmful consequences of integrating an *inflated, negative view of self.* Patients do need to consider improper behavior and negative views of self *when they are warranted.* However, unrealistic views of self are problematic, and this happens when patients vilify and demonize themselves, or when they accept others' overly negative appraisals. In that case, the negative image needs to be corrected. Diminution training does this by building a *cognitive countering capacity,* an ability to challenge irrational, unrealistic thinking.

To do this, diminution thinking utilizes self-questioning. Patients first identify the rejecting party's view. Self-questions are then used to challenge that conceptualization. In essence, patients perform cognitive restructuring on themselves.

If there are substantial bad feelings about oneself after a rejection (a three or more on a scale from zero to five), then *self-support training,* especially *self-boosting,* needs to be incorporated into treatment. *Imagery* can be used along with self-boosting. For example:

> I am a plant and it has not rained in a while. The rain stands for love. Without that rain, I am drooping. The caring side of me takes a bucket of water and pours it over myself. I perk up. As the water pours over me, I think of my positive qualities and recite them. Saying those positive qualities at that time is like giving me love.

Another use of diminution thinking is to counter or reduce catastrophic thinking. It is helpful for patients who are anxiety prone and imagine awful events as a result of rejection. Cognitive restructuring certainly is helpful for countering anxiogenic thinking, but it needs to be supplemented by learned self-questioning that can counter the irrational tendency to catastrophize. Some examples of self-questions:

- Where is my evidence to support this prediction that dire consequences will occur from this rejection?
- How do I know this dire consequence will occur?
- If it should occur, what can I do about it?
- What are alternative ways to cope with this dire consequence?

DISAPPOINTMENT ACCOMMODATION TRAINING

Every relationship contains either an overt or covert, conscious or unconscious, formative contract that stipulates the exchanges between parties: as long as you do this for me, I will continue doing that for you (Homans, 1967). People will continue certain behaviors (e.g., acting pleasant) providing they produce a desired and expected effect (e.g., stimulating a spouse to act pleasant in return). The reinforcers that build the relationship cement the ties between parties. As long as they continue in effect, the relationship has a bond that ties parties together. For example, "I will remain loyal to you in this marriage as long as you are a certain kind of spouse." However, as Homans (1974) points out, people will feel angry and stop performing a desired behavior when the rewards cease (e.g., the spouse stops acting pleasant due to chronic pain). When behavior ceases to be rewarded as usual, this lessens commitment to the relationship.

Chronic and terminal illness profoundly alters the formative contracts. In the crisis phase, relationships generally remain stable due to hope that the disease can be contained or eradicated. Even though the disease causes the patient to violate the basic contracts, loyalty to the relationship generally remains in effect. Uncertainty about what will happen next produces a "wait and see" attitude.

However, as the disease continues, family members, friends, and employers may not be able to accommodate and adjust to the changes. The contract between parties is unavoidably violated too many times by the infirm patient, who is not able to provide reinforcing behavior enough of the time. At the same time, the limitations of medical intervention become better known; what medicine or surgery can and cannot cure are better understood. The hope for a cure wanes. The long-term negative effects of the disease and their impact on role functioning become clearer. Realizing that many of the unwanted changes in the relationship will become permanent, discontent with medical patients rise when they cannot fulfill role duties. Support gives way to criticism; loyalty is replaced by disenchantment. Commitment to the relationship dissipates or evaporates. Willingness to preserve old role obligations and services diminishes.

In essence, disease removes basic reinforcers that hold the formative contract together. When this occurs, there is less willingness to uphold one's end of the contract. Spouses walk away. Friends pull away. Employers end employment. In summary, in the post-crisis phase, there are many changes in long-term relationships that cause medical patients to be frequently disappointed in others. In fact, disappointment becomes a constancy in the lives of chronic and terminally ill patients. Numerous relationships are suddenly or gradually altered or disintegrate with the advent of disease. Each disappointment produces a measure of sadness and grief that often turns to depression or rage. The plethora of disappointments can then lead to bitterness.

Providers will need to explain these changes to patients so they have an academic understanding of why others are not meeting their needs or are acting differently. This explanation does not excuse others from not fulfilling their contracts, though. It merely provides an understanding for why they have changed.

Cognition can complicate this problematic situation. Sparked by helplessness to secure what is wanted from others, there is a tendency to engage in imperative thinking: "He must meet my needs and not disappoint me any further." This demand for no more disappointment only acts to increase the level of frustration when others fail to satisfy the demand. Another problematic belief is the assertion that a given behavior is vital. This dramatically escalates the importance of someone performing a particular action. Not satisfying an expectation that is considered vital makes the consequence all the more painful. This influences the evaluation of the situation to such a degree that it may be seen as awful.

Oppositely, what would be a rational way chronic and terminally ill patients could think? Providers need to inculcate this way of thinking.

My disease has altered the basis for my relationships with others. It has changed the contract that supported the relationship. I cannot achieve desired outcomes by others. This will affect their behavior toward me. They will disappoint me as a result. I need to accommodate to the fact that others will disappoint me. That will happen and has to be accepted. I am not to blame for their not doing what I dearly desire. The disease is to blame, causing me not to be my old self.

This way of thinking has a twofold benefit. First, it correctly defines the reality that *disappointment will be an inevitable feeling amongst chronic and terminally ill patients and cannot be avoided.* Second, it prepares patients for changes in their relationships and disappointments when they arise. The overall message is that patients need to *allow for disappointment as a by-product of disease.*

ROLE OF COGNITIVE RESTRUCTURING

If patients have a difficult time accommodating to disappointment, then cognitive restructuring (CR) can be helpful. It can form a realistic appraisal about other people. Disappointment is, in part, a consequence of expectation. If the expectation for other's behavior is unrealistic, then the degree of disappointment will be greater. CR will expose those unrealistic expectations. It will focus on utilizing knowledge of other's personality and past history to form reasonable expectations of what others will or won't do. Specifically, once a patient declares that a significant other possesses certain qualities or features, then the patient should not be surprised when those features surface. For example: if a wife knows her husband is self-centered (a prototypical feature of that person), and he especially becomes upset when she does not reward him with desired behavior, then she should not be surprised when he becomes angry with her when she is too ill to do what he wants. In essence, self-centered people are like that. That's to be expected. A white wall will be a white wall and should not be expected to be green, even if someone dearly wants that wall to be green. In essence, CR asks patients to come to terms with prototypical features of a category. The husband (the category) has prototypical features (self-centeredness). When that feature is manifested it should be expected. The feature is part of the category and inseparable from it.

A second function of CR is correcting absolutistic thinking, specifically that certain actions of others are imperative and vital. CR would declare that a given action is only desirable and not crucial, preferable but not vital. Thinking that way, when disappointment does occur, there is less consternation.

CONSTRUCTIVE MOURNING

The focus on accepting reality as it is will bring patients closer to a basic feeling of loss that accompanies disappointment. Chronic and terminally ill patients live with an undercurrent of grief due to the harsh, unyielding reality that grips their lives. A change of thinking in cognitive restructuring may not be able to loosen that grip. Instead, many medical patients need to spend time addressing their sadness and sorrow about the many disappointments they face. A time for mourning is often necessary at various junctures in treatment, and cognitive-behavioral therapists ought to set aside time for that, or else accumulated disappointments will eventuate into bitterness. Historically, CR has not given time for grieving, and by not doing so can prolong treatment. Patients may not be able to move on until they have felt their grief, and not just cogitated about it.

In fact, there are many patients who need to process their emotions and talk about how events have affected them, before they can use others' advice, engage in intellectual discussion about their losses, and problem-solve. These people are emotionally oriented. Negative feelings will linger and can overwhelm them unless feelings are expressed. Martin and Doka (2000) have referred to them as *intuitive grievers.*

However, CR is a good choice for another group of patients Martin and Doka (2000) refer to as *instrumental grievers.* These are patients who objectively look at their losses, seek to understand why they have occurred, and want quickly to engage in problem-solving. This group of patients feels uncomfortable talking about their emotions or has little need to do so. Instead, they cogitate about their emotions and immerse themselves in activities as their way to cope. Intellectually examining their feelings in CR would be helpful and knowing how to change thinking complicating sorrow would be of interest to them.

Taking the different grieving styles into consideration, CCT has developed a method of grieving called **constructive mourning** that works with both the emotions and the intellect. It gives substantial time to both. It wants the intuitive griever to benefit from the intellect and at the same time it wants to facilitate the customary response of instrumental grievers, while giving them an opportunity to express their emotions if they so choose. Constructive mourning facilitates the resources within the patient, building potential capacities that can aid the bereaved. The technique *constructs parts of self that produce input into the grieving process* and aids adaptation to loss. By doing so, disappointment, while existing as a given, will not hurt so much.

To show how this approach works in actuality, a dialogue with a patient is provided. In the dialogue the therapist works to *construct "voices" within the patient to address grief.* Sherri, a chronic fatigue syndrome patient, is depressed about how her employer is responding to her. Sherri's career and her relationship with her boss, Jack, have been extremely important to her, but he has changed since her illness started. Distancing himself from her, he is no longer supportive of her work and is more critical. Repeatedly disappointed in how he acts has caused her to feel grief and bitterness. Sherri is an intuitive griever who tends to become mired in her emotions. The therapist wants to help her integrate her intellect into the grieving process, but not before he first connects to her emotional side, the dominant part of self. To do this he facilitates emotional expression.

Sherri (S):	I am so angry with my boss. He hardly talks to me these days. I know he would like me to quit because I am not as productive as I used to be, but I can't quit. We need the money and the health insurance. I used to love working for him but not anymore.
Therapist (T):	You are disappointed in your boss, for not being as he used to be.
S:	Yes, I am disappointed in him. He knows that I do what I can, but I am not as productive as the other adjusters. That bothers me a lot.
T:	I can see why you feel disappointed. You try your best, but it's not good enough for him. You want to please him, but you can't, because of your illness.
S:	Yes, it's very frustrating. He assigns me work that is far below my capacity. It's insulting.
T:	You feel put-down by how he is dealing with you.
S:	Very much so.
T:	I think you have a lot of grief about how things have changed at work. You care about your work a great deal and take a lot of pride in what you do. But it's not good enough for him anymore. That hurts you.
S:	(Sherri shakes her head and is teary-eyed.)

The dialogue to this point uses a client-centered, expressive-emotive technique to highlight and intensify the patient's feelings (Rogers, 1961; Rice and Greenberg, 1991). The therapist now moves on to construct other response capacities in a dialogic manner, as is done in Gestalt therapy (Polsters, 1973).

T:	There is a thinking part of you that sees your situation. It has ideas about the situation you are in. Become that part for the moment. What would that part say to the disap-

pointed part of you who feels so letdown by her boss?

S: (first unsure of what to say) Well, I guess I would say this guy is only caring about the company's money. Everything for him is bottom-line. I don't put out enough work so I cost the company money.

T: (as boss) You don't produce, so you will get the cold shoulder from me.

S: Yeah, that's right.

T: How would the part of you that feels disappointed respond to that?

S: I am angry about that. It's not right. It's not fair. I didn't want to have this damn disease, but I try to do my best at work even when I feel so drained.

T: Answer back as the thinking part of you. What are its thoughts about this problem?

S: Well, Jack (the boss) is like that. He's friendly when he wants something from you, but don't give him what he wants and he is a real cold fish.

       (The therapist wants to use her intellect to gain objectivity.)

T: You feel the coldness now and that saddens you (speaking to the emotional part of Sherri).

S: Yes, I like how he used to be pleased with me.

T: And now that is lost to you. (Sherri shakes her head dejectedly). Become the thinking part of you again. The emotional part of you feels the grief from the changes at work due to the fatigue that DOES NOT GO AWAY. How would you advise her?

S: Know you aren't going to please him. You would have to be your old self and that isn't going to happen, because this fatigue isn't going away anytime soon. (Sherri then switches to the emotional part of herself.) Yes, but that's what makes me so upset. I am so sick of being tired all the time and not doing my best at work.

T: I hear how much that means to you, losing that part of you that was such a good worker whom your boss respected so much. (Sherri shakes her head sadly in agreement.) It hurts being on the outs with Jack, when you used to be very close to him.

S: Yes, it is. I feel like I don't belong at work anymore.

T: What can the thinking part of you say about that?

S: You aren't going to get Jack's approval. You aren't going to be one of Jack's favorites anymore. That's just the way it is.

T: Answer back to that. Can the feeling part of you accept that?

S: Not very well, but I know I have to. I have to accept the changes at work even though I hate what's happened. (Sherri breathes more easily and shakes her head, as if she is agreeing with what she just said.)
        (By using Sherri's intellect to aid the grieving process, she appears to have moved forward in working through some of her grief. The therapist now moves to construct another response capacity to aid the grief work, an inspiring role model.)

T: Because of your illness, you have been forced to make many adjustments. Who in your life has had to make many hard adjustments and did it well? Have you known anyone who has suffered losses but coped with them well?

S: I would say my mother. She had many health problems in the later years of her life but handled herself very well. I was very proud of her.

T: Become your mother for the moment and have her talk to the feeling part of you that is so disappointed by how things are turning out at work.

S: I guess Mom would say that we have to move on. She was like that. She did not stay stuck in spilled milk.

T: What does the feeling part of you have to say about what Mom just said to you?
        (The dialogue continues on with Sherri becoming her mother and dialoging with the feeling part of Sherri. The purpose is to encourage her to copy the actions of the role model. Later in the session, the therapist uses the voice of Sherri's mother to advise her about how to feel when Jack is cold to her.)

In this dialogue, the therapist has constructed three response capacities. First, the emotional part of her was able to express feelings and ventilate. The intellect then provided an objective, reasoning response to those feelings. Sherri's mother provides a third voice, and she is used to inspire and motivate. By using the intellect and the role model, the therapist not only helps Sherri express her feelings, but allows her to become more objective. This objectivity helps her to emotionally work through troubled feelings.

Eventually the therapist also creates a fourth part of self. He joins the intellect and role model to forge a "goal state voice." This is a reasonable, practical part of self who is adaptive. It embodies whom Sherri would like to become at work, given her physical limitations. This is a person who takes pride in whatever she does, because it is her best effort. It does not disparage efforts when she does not meet Jack's expectations. The therapist then uses the goal-state voice as a portable resource, to advise Sherri at work or anywhere about how to think and feel when she feels sad.

SELF-INSTRUCTION TRAINING

In the above approach, a self-dialogue is created to guide responses to disappointment. The intellect and the goal-state are parts of Sherri not previously used. They can modify her emotional reactions and prepare her for possible disappointments. Each of those voices can become part of a self-instruction dialogue, which can be blended in with constructive mourning. The following self-talk was prepared for Sherri. It focuses on *disappointment tolerance.*

"Other people are not what I want them to be. That makes me feel sad, but I have to live with that sadness. I can tolerate it.

I need to get used to disappointments and adjust to them. I have had many and will have more.

Disappointment with others feels bad, but I can tolerate it.

I can work to get others to treat me the way I want, but they may not meet my needs. I have to be ready to accept that reality.

Tolerate their disapproval of me. I'm still okay regardless.

I would like to be my old self at work, but I cannot be that way.

I may disappoint others, but I have to bear that.

When I feel disappointed, take some deep breaths. Relax. Don't get uptight.

Disappointing others does not make me bad."

Summary

Bitterness is a common feeling in chronic and terminal illness patients. The bitterness experience contains feelings of resentment and disillusionment. Cognitive restructuring maintains that irrational, erroneous thinking—in particular, imperative thinking and severe evaluations of the situation—cause that emotion. Two causes of bitterness are studied: rejection and disappointment. Coping skills for each are given. Rejection tolerance includes such skills as reality detection, acceptance training, identity scrutiny, and diminution training. Disappointment accommodation features the skill of constructive mourning in combination with self-instruction training.

Body Accommodation and Disfigurement Neutralization

> I tell my body to get going, but it won't move. I tell my hands
> to open something, but they cannot move the object. I am so
> disgusted with myself.
>
> —Deborah, arthritis patient

P eople have a historical relationship with their bodies, where the
body is supposed to be the service provider. The self sets goals
and the body is supposed to meet those goals. The self sets a
standard for how a job is supposed to be carried out (at a certain speed
or in a certain way) and the body is supposed to meet that standard.
The self has a conceptualization of how the body should appear and
the body is supposed to fulfill that conceptualization. The self knows
how it wants the body to feel and the body is supposed to feel that way.
In summary, the body is told to measure up and accommodate what
the self wants from it. Certainly there are times where this relationship
is reversed (e.g., when the body becomes sleepy or feels a need to
urinate and the self responds by going to bed or the bathroom), but
by and large the historical relationship stays in effect. By and large, the
body is given the task to conform to what the self wants, and not
vice versa.

But with symptom onset and the treatment for it, the body becomes
less capable of being a service provider in several' regards. Early patience
with the body that cannot perform up to par is in time replaced with
impatience as individuals move into the postcrisis phase. At this time,
many patients have a most difficult time coping with permanent or
recurring changes in physical functioning. Some assume a normalization coping strategy and demand that their body conforms to customary
standards and expectations. It is put down for not looking or acting as

expected. Irregularity is not tolerated. Incapacity is met with chagrin, disdain, and embarrassment. Dysfunction is rejected, repudiated, and the body is held to task. An estrangement between self and body occur, where the former becomes an antagonist to the latter.

To reunify person and body, the former has to accommodate to alterations in the latter. A way has to be found to make peace with a condition far less than desirable. This chapter provides guidelines for doing this. In particular, it presents treatment for rejection of the body when it is considered disfigured.

THE COGNITIVE RESTRUCTURING APPROACH

Cognitive restructuring (CR) offers one way to heal alienation from the body. It would treat the unwillingness to be accommodating to bodily changes by disputing the belief set of the patient. The distress about the body is conceived as a cognitive problem.

In essence, *CR works to soften harsh thinking.* It makes rigid, harsh, demanding thinking featuring "musts" and "have to's" more flexible ("It would be better if . . . "). It seeks changes by degree, where someone becomes less condemning, less demanding, more patient, more accommodating. It wants patients to realize the adverse effects of their thinking on their situation, so they do not make a bad situation even worse. Over all, CR wants patients to develop a healing philosophy toward their body in the following way:

- Deal with the body as it is and not how you wish it to be. Accept it as it is.
- Don't set unreasonable standards for it. Consider its limitations.
- Don't rate the body. Ratings will only cause more problems.
- Don't compare the body with how it used to be or to other people's bodies.

While CR does have merit as an intervention, it does not go far enough in developing needed responses to the body. While it changes how the person relates to his/her body, so there is less anger, it does not do enough to build roles and mental manners required for living with an infirm, ill body. Instead, CR needs to be supplemented by a response set that is called *body accommodation.* This will lead into the consolidation phase, when self-alienation is overcome and the person is rejoined with his or her body. It facilitates living with or co-existing with a form, look, or mechanical process that is neither liked nor wanted.

THE BODY ACCOMMODATION APPROACH

Body accommodation builds on the ideas of self-support training (discussed in Chapter 7). It alters the historical relationship with the body. It requires the patient to assume a certain attitude and engage in certain activities regarding the body. It wants patients to do the following (the list below is a handout on the disc):

1. Become willing to be a service provider to your body, to oblige your body by meeting its needs when there is fatigue, weakness, or pain requiring rest or medication.
2. Grant yourself permission—without feeling guilty, remorse, or shame—not to meet standards or expectations when they are unreasonable. Place only realistic expectations on your body.
3. Support yourself by becoming an advocate for your body when others are critical or lack understanding of how you are.
4. *Accept your physical limitations* and work with others to help them accept your physical limitations. Reconcile with the critical part of yourself who seeks a different body. Adjust to a less than satisfactory effort.
5. Extend consideration to yourself when your body shows a limitation. Do not lambaste it or show disdain when it cannot perform as desired. Treat it courteously and politely. Extend graciousness to your body when it is not its "ol' self." Give your body respect and deference for its efforts. *Respond to it in a mannerly way.*
6. Show gratitude to your body for whatever it can do. Appreciate its efforts. Reinforce those efforts with such self-statements as, "I like how I am able to . . . "

As a rule, patients perform the first task but often fail to perform the last five, especially when feeling depressed or angry. For instance, many patients in pain may stop what they are doing, take a rest, and place heat or ice on their body to feel better, but internally feel irritated for needing to rest while there is still work to be done. Those same patients may take time to lie down but look at their body with disdain and shake their head in disbelief for why a task cannot be performed. Instead, the goal is maintaining body accommodation especially when there *is* impatience and intolerance with oneself. The intention is to treat body incapacity in a caring manner.

Therapists will need to show many examples of body accommodation, especially about how to be respectful and gracious toward the body. Examples of body rejection need to be given and compared to a body accommodation strategy. Patients can then decide which is best and most productive. (Example: "You are feeling fatigued. What would you say to yourself to show patience and respect, and what would you say if you felt disrespect toward your body?")

EDUCATION PHASE

The education phase about body accommodation needs to include the following:

1)   Secure the patient's appraisal of his body, including the feelings and thoughts about the changes since symptom onset and the beginning of treatment.
One way to do this is by completing a *body appraisal inventory*. To do this, go over each body part (i.e., nose, hands, breasts, etc.) and have the patient rate each part from zero to four (4 = excellent, 3 = good, 2 = average, 1 = below average, 0 = failing) before and after symptom onset. Add the score and divide by the number of body parts that were rated. This yields an overall appraisal of the body before and after symptom onset. The patient can also give thumbs-up or thumbs-down on the body, or give a sound to describe premorbid and postmorbid time periods (e.g., ahhhh, yich). If a patient rates most of his/her body parts as positive but has an overall negative rating of the whole body, then that reveals the dominance of a negative body image on the appraisal of self.
2)   Catalogue signs of rejection of bodily changes. Usually, the signs are subtle and nonverbal, such as deep sighs, disdainful looks, or a shaking head when an action is not completed. There can be affective signs, such as general irritability, impatience, or sadness when thinking about the body. Create a personal patient index or profile of the ways that the individual shows disrespect and rejection toward him/herself. Label those signs as unwillingness to accommodate to how the body is presently functioning.
3)   Ask the patient to monitor for those signs of rejection. A log can be kept on a check-off form, where each sign is listed and the patient checks off any sign of rejection noticed that day.
4)   Discuss the pros and cons of body rejection. The drawbacks would include lowering of self-esteem and being susceptible to depression. The benefits would include venting of feeling and facilitation of protest against disease or the treatment program.

5)   Discuss the pros and cons of body accommodation. The patient is then asked which strategy s/he wishes to pursue, rejection or accommodation to changes in the body. This forces the patient to take responsibility for his/her attitude and behavior toward self.

TREATMENT

Once patients feel ready to discontinue body rejection, they then need an appropriate attitude toward the body, especially when it is incapable of meeting expectations. Self-instruction training can be used to develop that attitude. It should include the following:

a)   self-instructions to be said before an activity that is difficult to perform is undertaken, to avoid slipping into self-deprecation.
b)   sentences for when the activity is occurring, to maintain a positive attitude.
c)   sentences for when the body is not actually meeting expectations and anger is building.
d)   sentences to identify body accomplishments and encourage self-praise.

There are two goals in the self-dialogue. One is response prevention: to inhibit self-recrimination against the body. The other is response substitution: to create a substitute self-dialogue that facilitates accommodation of the body. Both of these goals are written into the self-dialogue below (on disc***), developed for a patient who suffers from weakness and tremor.

Self-Dialogue Before the Body Undertakes a Task

What do I have to do in this situation? What will be hard for my body?

Figure out a plan for how to do the job.

What are reasonable expectations for my body in this situation?

Don't get upset with myself when I feel weak. Be patient.

This is how I am now. Accept that fact.

Show respect and be supportive of whatever the body can do.

Don't demand the body be like its old self. I am different now. Accept that fact.

Self-Dialogue When the Activity Is Undertaken

I will do what I can. Don't get down on myself for not doing more.

My body has changed, so it may not do what it used to do.

Easy does it. Don't be pushy.

Show understanding of whatever the body can do.

Be gracious when the body has to stop its work.

Thank it for its effort. Comment on what was done well or what was completed.

Do as much as I can but don't overdo it.

Don't be self-critical. Don't look for faults with performance. Don't be impatient.

Do a piece of work and gradually it will get done.

Self-Dialogue When the Body Cannot Perform

I feel angry now. How much anger do I feel, from 0 to 5?

What are other signs of body rejection?

Don't be angry at the body. Be understanding.

I cannot meet old standards. I don't have a bad body, just a different one than I used to have.

I am not a machine. I do what I can do. I do the best I can do.

Show appreciation for what's been done. Show caring toward my effort.

Plan how to complete the rest of the project.

Where is it written that I have to complete everything all at once?

Don't get into awfulizing. It's not terrible to be tired. It's just not preferable.

Self-Dialogue After Completing an Activity

Do I have any resentment toward myself?

Look at what I did well and praise my efforts

Don't look at what was not done well.

Don't hold the body to unreasonable standards.

THE SENSE OF DISFIGUREMENT

Besides the need to reorient the patient to accommodate to changes in the body, there is another need to accommodate to changes in anatomy and appearance that are perceived as disfigurement. For instance, viral hepatitis patients need to accommodate to yellowing of the skin and bloating of the stomach. Rheumatoid arthritis patients must adjust to changes in their joints (hands, feet) and back. There are also changes in appearance due to the treatment for various diseases. For example, mastectomy patients have to confront changes in the female form. Cancer patients often have to endure loss of hair and a healthy appearance. Patients who have had surgery must accommodate to scar tissue that may cover large areas of their body. Amputees must also deal with loss of limb.

Whenever there are anatomy or appearance changes, people will naturally conceptualize that change. One pejorative conceptualization defines the person as disfigured. In this case the body or body part *is viewed as deformed, spoiled, or misshapen.* It is labeled as flawed and no longer representing a healthy appearance, that person's self-image, or society's image of the male or female body.

The sense of disfigurement is subjective, for an actual alteration in body appearance or anatomy need not lead to a feeling of disfigurement. For example, a mastectomy need not automatically cause a women to feel flawed, but it will if she believes that the female form must include two natural breasts, and if they are not present, then she is something less than a woman. Hence, to arrive at a self-definition of disfigurement, there needs to be a cognitive-affective process. First, a value judgment is made where a new rating of the self downgrades the body. At the same time a judgment about meaning is formulated that defines the body as disfigured. Reductionist thinking then occurs, equating the person to the diminished self-rating. For example, a woman equates the loss of her breast(s) to a lower level of femininity and attractiveness. The other qualities that support femininity are discounted or ignored. Affectively, this cognitive process influences the emotional response, causing a feeling of dislike or hatred of the altered appearance.

The first step in treating disfigurement is to *secure the patient's definition of the change in bodily appearance.* Ask the patient to describe her altered body, with as many words as possible. Divide the answers between descriptive and evaluative words. For example, words like hideous, ugly, or misshapen are evaluative words. They contain an implied continuum that rates a body part from high to low in goodness. Hence, there is not a state of ugliness, but ugliness on a continuum from slightly ugly to severely ugly. Compile a rating of each evaluative word (from 0 to 4) to learn how negative the patient is about his/her body. In regard to the descriptive words, find other words that are neutral or even positive to describe the same body part. Inquire if the patient would use those words and if not, why not.

If the patient subscribes to a list of pejorative, demeaning descriptions and evaluations for the body, *inquire if s/he feels disfigured* by the disease or the treatment for it, to corroborate the self-diagnosis. If the answer is affirmative, then ask how that view of self shapes the emotional response.

If the patient feels disfigured, then inquire what must occur to form a better definition of self. Essentially, what/would make the patient feel whole again and no longer stained or damaged? This will provide information on whether a magical ending is required to feel better, such as a return to the old form or anatomy. For instance, the breast or testicle that were removed would have to be returned in a healthy state. In essence, history would have to be wiped away in order to erase the disfigurement.

Relay to the patient that a definition of disfigurement is actually a severe, extreme, disguised negative evaluation of the body or a body part. Gain corroboration if the patient does consciously, objectively rate his/her body or body parts as awful in appearance or form. Inquire if the patient sees him/herself as inferior to others, and if the body is held in disdain.

CCT does not regard self-disdain as unusual, strange, or a sign of pathology. On the contrary, it believes that virtually all medical patients show some degree of it when there have been changes in bodily appearance or anatomy. The treatment issue is managing or neutralizing that sense of disfigurement so it does not cause further suffering. To accomplish that task, CCT uses a series of skills collectively called disfigurement neutralization.

DISFIGUREMENT NEUTRALIZATION

Disfigurement neutralization is an ability to neutralize the negative evaluation of the body's appearance or anatomy. The method concedes that disease will change the body for the worse, and that there will be some degree of negative feeling that can be overcome or diluted with the aid of certain skills. However, before putting those skills into place, therapists will need to address how patients think about themselves.

The sense of disfigurement is often difficult to change and treat because patients are convinced that they are flawed and deformed. They have the unshakable belief that they are inadequate and perversely unique, when compared with others. Their belief set is:

- I am not like other people now, due to this disease (or treatment).
- I cannot be accepted if I am unlike everyone else.
- Because of my body's condition I am not worth as much as others.
- My difference from others will be noticed and cause me to be branded as a freak.
- Others will not be able to overlook my undesirable body (or body part), and they will stay negatively focused on me.
- Others will not want to get involved with me because I am so different, causing me to be eventually rejected.

These beliefs become problematic because they exist as fixed perceptions that CCT labels certainistic thinking. In working with the disfigured, the therapist sees that they not only have unrealistic thinking, but also unyielding confidence in their unrealistic thoughts.

Cognitive restructuring (CR) would ask patients for their data to support these ideas. However, many times certain thinkers will have little or no data to support their thinking, but will still cling to their unrealistic ideas. A coping skills approach could address this problem through *doubtfulness training*. First, patients are confronted that they are a true believer. They need to be aware of how they think, that their mental process is biased and they mistrust other points of view. They need to be aware that their thinking is invalid and will lead to negative consequences (but they will not see that because they have faith in their inaccurate thinking).

To feel better about themselves, patients are then asked to deliberately doubt their own judgments and mistrust their own thinking. To do this, patients need to be willing to accept the possibility that their judgments could be inaccurate. They need to be willing to adopt a mental format for working with their beliefs. This means not automatically buying a way of thinking, and to remain skeptical of their own conclusions.

After noticing a bad feeling about themselves, they are asked to automatically hesitate to accept a pejorative view of self. Next, to encourage *objectivity*, they are asked to see themselves through other people's eyes. They pretend to be another person whom they respect. Then, speaking to themselves as that other person, present to the patient the other person's thoughts and views of self. Homework is given to cast doubt on their thinking several times a day, and then rate how well they are doing at doubting themselves.

Part of the reason patients have such a fixed, negative viewpoint is not only because of irrational thinking, but because they are so dejected and filled with sorrow about the current state of their body. They feel an immense loss over what their body has become. When they are able to mourn the loss of their old body or any ideal body they will never achieve due to disease, they are better able to benefit from a CR approach. They can entertain logical arguments when they are not so impacted with negative emotion. Mourning eases painful feelings.

CONSTRUCTIVE MOURNING

There are several layers to painful feelings. One feeling is connected to another, which is connected to still another. Quite often depression is the first layer that is encountered, and under that is anger that takes the form of aggression (Jacobson, 1971). Involved in that anger is narcissistic disillusionment that the body is not what it used to be. The outlet for the disillusionment becomes self-hatred and self-castigation. Adding to the aggression is a profound helplessness that little can be done about the situation (Bibring, 1953).

Behind the anger, dejection is often encountered. It occurs when there has been a breakdown in self-regard and healthy narcissism. Unwanted bodily changes feel like an insult to the narcissistic configuration (e.g., having two healthy breasts, testicles, arms, or legs). That configuration that everyone seeks appears lost. When dejection over this narcissistic insult is encountered, therapists should explain what is healthy narcissism, how bodily changes are experienced as an insult to it, and how that feeling of insult lowers self-esteem.

The focus at this point is to move patients beyond their rage and aggression, so they can encounter the flip side of their rage—the dejection, sadness, and sorrow about the loss of the narcissistic ideal (of having an acceptable body). This method seeks to connect the patient to disowned emotions. Another method to facilitate the expression of anger is through a dialogic technique (Polsters, 1973). The patient speaks with the disfigured body and then the patient becomes the body and replies.

Letter writing (Diamond, 2000) is an alternative to a dialogic tactic. A patient may be asked to write a letter to the part of him/herself that feels angry and dejected about the disfigured body or body part. The letter may be written to God or fate to express anger about becoming sick. Letter writing can also be used to facilitate a realistic perspective. For example, the patient can be asked to become fate and write a letter back to gain objectivity ("I, fate, play no favorites. I don't get involved with fairness. I can visit anyone's life with a disease at anytime.").

Once anger is softened, the strategy can then shift to mourning the loss of body functioning, body tissue, or desired appearance. For grief work, CCT uses the technique of constructive mourning. It makes use of parts of self to facilitate resolution. To illustrate how parts of self are used for treating disfigurement and body accommodation, a case study follows.

Judith was a mastectomy patient in her early forties who had one of her breasts removed. The therapist constructed two other parts of self to work with her emotions. One was her intellect, to give her an objective view of her situation. The therapist also wanted to develop an inspiring, supportive part of self that could speak to her, motivate her, and buoy her spirits. To develop the inspiring part of self, Judith was asked who had been an inspiration for her in her life. That person could then become her role model. Judith chose her aunt, whom she had admired since childhood. The aunt also had breast cancer.

When Judith would feel frightened or unattractive, each of the two parts of self would be commissioned to speak to her. Judith was trained to give life to these parts of self who would then work to treat her emotions containing the hurt, anger, and sadness. To adequately construct these other parts of self, the therapist first spoke to Judith about her emotions. After giving her time to express her feelings, the therapist asked her to become another part of self and answer back. To facilitate their viewpoints, the therapist role-played the alter ego for her intellect and inspiring parts. Judith listened to the comments of these other parts to learn how they could address her situation.

The key to using this technique is getting the patient to actually recognize that s/he does possess other viewpoints embodied in other parts of self. Giving them a voice facilitates a conceptual shift. It also provides the patient with other ways to manage the situation.

For example, with Judith taking on the role of her intellect, she was asked the following questions:

- What do you think about getting cancer?
- What do you think when you have negative feelings about how you look?
- What do you think about your response to losing your breast?

- How do you think a mastectomy patient can cope with her situation?
- When you feel odd or ugly because of your mastectomy, what are your thoughts at that time?
- When you assume that people pity you or look at you as a freak, with only one breast, what are your thoughts at that time?

Judith was also asked to role-play her aunt to learn how she, acting as that role model, could be used to inspire Judith. In the role of her aunt she was asked:

- What kind of person are you? How are you and Judith alike?
- Judith said that you had rough times in your life. How did you cope during those times?
- What do you think about Judith?
- When does she feel down and what makes her feel sad?
- What can you say to her at those times that would be helpful?
- How have you coped when you felt dejected, especially if you felt that way after your mastectomy?
- Going back to times in your life when you felt different after your mastectomy, what did you do to manage your feelings?

Once the thoughts of these parts of self were revealed, the therapist acted as a moderator, asking Judith in her various roles to respond to the viewpoint of another role. For instance:

"What does the thinking part of you have to say about Judith's feeling of embarrassment?"

"How would your aunt respond to that way of thinking by the intellectual part of you? Does she agree with that thought?

"Hearing what your aunt said, how does the feeling part of you respond to that? Tell me about your emotions."

"Hearing Judith's feelings, what would the thinking part of you say? Offer Judith some advice?"

Once emotions about bodily changes have been lessened, medical patients are then better able to move into the next phase of disfigurement neutralization, which is acceptance training.

ACCEPTANCE

Acceptance training for body accommodation stresses openness to whatever the body is. This entails *living with and caring for who one is.* By doing so, acceptance overcomes the endless combat against oneself. It stops the hypercriticalness and self-derision commonly seen in the alienation phase, when patients bitterly denounce their life. Acceptance facilitates allowance of an upsetting, unwanted body. It encourages coexistence with that body. In time, acceptance encourages moving beyond tolerance of a disliked body to appreciating it. At that point, the self rejoins its corporeal form, moving into the consolidation phase.

The therapist will need to present the ideas of acceptance and how they can benefit the patient, as part of the induction into using the skill. Patients, though, may respond that their body is awful, but the therapist can counter that belief with the following prescription. "You are free to see yourself in an excessively negative light but still be accepting of yourself—if you are willing to embrace who you are, whatever you are. The goal is overcoming your unwillingness to live with your body as what it is. Certainly, you will have an easier time accepting yourself if you considered your body more positively than it is, or at least not as negatively. However, even if you evaluate your body very badly, you can still accept it and in time even care for what it can offer you."

Going against acceptance is the agonistic tendency to fight what the body has become and reject the corporeal form. The disfigured may even admit that their body is not the worst, but continue thinking of themselves that way. They can have a realistic view of themselves as "not that bad" but still think of themselves in a negative way. That is because a body part does not meet their standard: "I must be who I want to be, and anything else is not wanted." This absolutistic belief steadfastly pushes patients to demand their coveted ideal or desired standard, and unless that occurs there is discontent.

The cognitive-behavioral therapist can steadfastly treat this belief with cognitive restructuring. The following rational position is presented. "People cannot always get what they want in life. It would be desirable if I could, but not getting my way is not terrible, just unfortunate."

DISAPPOINTMENT ACCOMMODATION

However, CCT would maintain that patients need more than just rational thinking. They need skills to develop response capacities that can substitute for and diminish the self-rejecting strategy, while facilitating the acceptance response. With that aim in mind, the coping strategy of *disappointment accommodation* is presented to patients. When inducting the patient into using this skill, the therapist needs to acknowledge that the body will not meet the patient's standards and that disappointment will be the inevitable end result, as long as the standard for the body is in place. Obviously, one choice is abandoning the insensitive, demanding standard. But if the patient chooses not to do that, then the second option is learning to accommodate to disappointment in self and with life. That strategy will be necessary if the standard is preserved. This follows one of the basic therapeutic strategies of CCT: if patients are determined to pursue a coping strategy (rejection of the body) that results in a negative emotion, they will need to learn a skill to cope with the consequences from that decision.

A self-dialogue can then be developed to formulate the coping strategy such as:

This is not the body I wanted. I would like to be different, but I cannot be different.

I feel disappointed in myself and with my life. There is no way to avoid disappointment because I wanted a different situation, a different body.

Accept the disappointment. Live with it. It will be my reality, because I want some other type of body.

However, I do not have to continue to focus on what I am not. I can focus on other matters that will be more pleasing to me.

Don't fall into self-pity. No 'woe is me' thinking.

Move on and live with what I will not be. I can accommodate to this disappointment and overlook my body's shortcoming.

The self-dialogue has two benefits. One, it can help patients realize that their thinking is the actual cause of pain and not their body that is viewed as disfigured. But, if patients continue to seek the body they demand or dearly want, then disappointment accommodation can ease the fallout from that unwise decision.

Another way to change the agonistic tendency is by discussing a potential cause for rejecting the body. That cause is refusal to be impotent or helpless. Present to the patient the idea that behind his/her rage about having a disfigured body is a deep sadness about being impotent and unable to be "who you want to be." After giving time and encouragement to express that sadness, the coping skills therapist can then move the discussion to using the skill of *helplessness tolerance*, discussed in Chapter 12.

SYMBOLIC GESTURING

CCT uses another tactic to deal with body rejection. This tactic makes the body rejection strategy vivid, so it can be seen clearly as resistance against embracing reality. In work with patients who stubbornly cling to the perception that their body is disfigured, CCT asks them to practice a gesture that symbolizes what they are doing. This illuminates the maladaptive coping strategy, but in a dramatic way.

Here are two examples of symbolic gestures that were used with patients who rejected themselves. They were part of a paradoxical intervention that encouraged defiance against the therapist's instructions to accept oneself. The gesture forced the patient to exaggerate her position of body rejection, so it stands out more clearly. The technique is inspired by Gestalt therapy's exaggeration technique, which is a paradoxical tactic (Naranjo, 1980).

Sharon was a goiter patient with a massive distention and swelling of the neck. She felt ashamed of her appearance whenever she was out in public. While she had many other positive qualities, reductionistic thinking had caused her to equate her self-image with her altered appearance ("I equal my neck, I am unattractive"). Supportive therapy that featured self-boosting and self-compassion did little to raise her self-esteem. Therefore, her therapist recommended that she practice the following exercise when she thought of her body negatively. She was to form a disgusted look on her face, as if smelling rotting fish. She was to purse her lips and distort her expression. She then would have to put her hand over her eyes to hide from something that is revolting to her (the image of her upper body), while holding out her other hand to keep what is revolting away from her. She was to maintain this pose for a period of time as she imagined her appearance. When she grew tired of thinking of herself negatively, she could then switch body gestures to caress her neck and stroke it gently, to symbolize self-caring and self-acceptance. The exercise exaggerated her self-rejection so it could make an impression on her. While prescribing self-rejection, the intent was to inspire defiance against the prescription, to motivate her to seek self-acceptance.

In another example, Jeff, a teenager with cerebral palsy, felt disfigured by his involuntary movements: grimaces, wormlike writhing, and sharp jerks. The involuntary facial movements made his speech difficult to understand. These movements became more severe with stress, especially in school where he desperately wanted to be accepted. A vicious cycle developed. The more he worried about being accepted, the more he felt stressed, causing more involuntary movements that made him feel even more stressed. Therapy had failed to change his stubborn allegiance to his belief that he was undesirable. The therapist gave him a choice to continue to be disgusted with his appearance or accept who he was. Jeff wanted the latter but his disallowance of his condition caused him to mindlessly feel disgusted with himself. To facilitate self-acceptance, the therapist gave Jeff the following exercise to be performed several times a day.

"Hold out the palms of your hands as if you were keeping something away from you—the image of your body that you dislike so much. At the same time you are doing that, brace your face and other body muscles as if you are in a fight against something. Feel your hatred of how your body acts and looks at that time. When you tire of doing this, let out a long, deep breath and relax. Turn your palms upward and open them, as if you are receiving something. Receive a different view of yourself as a desirable person composed of many qualities, someone others would want to get to know, providing you can approach them without always thinking of yourself as a disfigured person."

The exercise concretized Jeff's fight against changing his negative thinking about himself. It brought to his attention the need to give up the unrealistic wish to be physically different than he was. It brought him to the critical crossroad he had to face: continue self-deprecation or accept himself as he was. The reverse gesture of opening his palms created readiness to change his view of self.

Once more ready to accept himself, other coping skills were used, along with symbolic gesturing, including self-boosting, relaxation techniques, *and* sensory diversion. *In regard to self-boosting, Jeff was told to list his good qualities and put each quality on a separate sheet of paper. He was to put these papers into his pockets and take them to school with him. When he felt insecure, he was to put his hands in his pockets and "feel" his good qualities.*

THERAPEUTIC STORYTELLING

Cognitive restructuring and coping skill development are direct ways to change thinking. They appeal to the conscious mind, where patients are aware of what the therapist is trying to do. These methods are useful for patients who are ready to change or at least ready to discuss their problems. However, there are patients who are defensive and ill-prepared to confront their problems in treatment. Their conscious mind is too guarded and frightened to deal with a topic head on. There may be too much fear of trying a particular behavior. Other patients may prefer to protest what has happened to them instead of seeking to change. Their anger is extensive, and they are unwilling at that moment to put it aside. With such patients, resistance is extensive and defeats turn aside resiliency.

To help these patients, an indirect and subtle method, metaphorical storytelling, can be tried (Gordon, 1978; Gordon and Meyers-Anderson, 1981). In this method, the therapist simply chitchats with the patient. This lowers the patient's guard, assuming that only small talk is going on, while in actuality challenging ideas are being presented to the unconscious mind. A metaphor embedded in the story bypasses the conscious mind and influences the unconscious. Included in the story are disguised solutions and treatment recommendations. The story can either present an alternative way of thinking or operating, or suggest a counter to the patient's way of thinking. Hence, the method can change thinking without having to use formal disputation tactics as in cognitive restructuring.

Steps for therapeutic storytelling:

1.   Identify the relationship the patient has with other people, e.g., if it is a relationship among equals or where one feels subordinate to others.

2.   Tell a story where the details parallel the patient's situation. An isomorphic relationship between characters in the story and characters in the patient's real life needs to be preserved. The story preserves the relationship between the people in the patient's life. For example, a wagon-train master may symbolize the father, and the patient, the first son, is the scout, going out to explore the world on the direction of the wagon-train master.

3.   The story needs to contain goals, where it moves in a certain direction (e.g., win a game). The story may contain a metaphor for what the patient has done in the past that has not worked, and a metaphor for what can work in the future.

4.   Included in the story is a resolution to a problem (e.g., winning a game). The story offers a new strategy to achieve a desired outcome.

Below is an example of therapeutic storytelling with Mark, a single, young adult whose world revolved around dating and being a lady's man, until he developed testicular cancer. He felt disfigured by the removal of his testicles and bitter that his manliness rested on hormone replacement. He felt devastated and highly inadequate that he no longer came "fully equipped." Feeling inferior to other males, he refused to date any longer and became depressed. Direct methods of changing his thinking such as behavioral therapy and cognitive restructuring were unsuccessful. He was too hesitant to discuss his true thoughts about himself and denied his emotions, declaring that he was doing fine coping with his loss. Yet, he remained too fearful and embarrassed to approach women, who used to be the center of his life.

Using therapeutic storytelling, the therapist found a subject Mark was interested in, which was sports. The session began with small talk about recent games. The therapist told the story of a game involving a major college basketball power, the University of Maryland, and a small college. "Did you read about the game Maryland played against Towson University?" the therapist inquired. "This little school that's not on the same level as Maryland really played them tough. Maryland really had its hands full with Towson." The therapist went on to discuss other David and Goliath sports events.

Through the sports stories, the therapist indirectly proposed a way of thinking, that Mark could still be a most formidable male suitor even while lacking natural equipment. The metaphors indirectly worked to change Mark's thinking that he was no longer competitive with other "superior" males in gaining the favor of women. The therapist maintained the relationship Mark had with other males—a vertical relationship where Mark saw himself as inferior to other males. The therapist did not want to dispute that notion at that moment because Mark was not ready to surrender his thinking. While preserving Mark's view of reality, it nevertheless challenged it, by saying that Towson U., a small college unequal to a big-time ACC power, could still produce big results.

As Mark began to progress in therapy and felt somewhat better about himself, other story lines were proposed by the therapist that built and transformed Mark's sullied self-image.

"I was reading about that football game between Ohio State and Southern Cal. It was nice watching these two great powers with long football traditions play each other. Cal used this unusual offense that really worked against Ohio State. You don't see that offense very often. Cal did very well against Ohio State. I give the coach of Southern Cal a lot of credit. He tried something different that is not seen very often. He wasn't afraid to fail. He had confidence in his players and game plan. I liked that."

The metaphor of two powerhouses playing each other was used because Mark was ready to hear that he was equal to other males. While the metaphor paced Mark's progress, it also led him in a desired direction. While he was starting to date, he continued to feel frightened about approaching women sexually. The metaphor helped move him along further to be more adventurous and take on risks. The metaphor made the point that he could win like Southern Cal with a "different" way of playing.

While Mark was aware that hormones and cosmetic surgery could make him appear as good as other males, he still was horrified by rejection from women. He feared that when they learned he could not father children they would not want him. Again, a sports metaphor was used to help him accept himself.

"Did you see that Maryland game? Juan Dixon really killed North Carolina. He's a great player. Even though he is not as big as other guards or even as naturally talented in many ways as other players Maryland has had, Juan does have heart, is a very hard worker, has his own game, his own style, and the fans love him. Bigger and more talented players do not intimidate him. He takes the game to them. I am sure he'll make it in the pros as soon as some coach gives him a chance. The fans will demand that they play him, once they get to know his game."

Again, the story was isomorphic to Mark's situation. In the story he was portrayed as an individual who succeeds because he perseveres, is not intimidated, and has many fine qualities that can make him a success with a future pro coach and fans—metaphors for women whom he would want to know. The story provides Mark with a potential optimistic, happy ending to his situation, that even though he could not father children, women might still find his overall qualities attractive enough to make him their beau or husband. The story also gives Mark a role model, someone who is lacking in certain regards (e.g., lack of size) but triumphs in the end.

Metaphorical storytelling was a way to overcome disappointment with oneself indirectly. It also promoted self-boosting indirectly, while raising his self-esteem. It prepared Mark for direct methods of therapy like cognitive restructuring. It laid the groundwork for open discussions of his problems.

Summary

Body accommodation is practiced to make a patient into a service provider to the body in need of help. Involved in this are permission-giving to be different, self-support, self-consideration, and gratitude for what the body can offer. Self-instructions can facilitate this mind-set. There are other patients who cannot accommodate what the body has become because they see it as disfigured.

Disfigurement is a value placed on the body that it is deformed, spoiled, or misshapen. Disfigurement neutralization is practiced when someone feels deformed. Constructive mourning is employed to address the underlying grief about losing the old body or an ideal body. Acceptance is practiced to live with what the body has become. If a patient continues to reject her body, symbolic gesturing can be used to illuminate that stance. Some patients cannot readily discuss the issue of disfigurement, so therapeutic storytelling can be used with them.

Part IV

Coping Skills
for Consolidation Phase

Chapter 11

Meaning-Making

> I just did not know what to do with myself after I went on disability. What free time I had seemed to be spent in doctors' offices. I had very little going for myself.
>
> —Bruce, angina patient

Meaning-making addresses the problem of how to cope with transitions, the time between formed states of being. Prior to symptom onset, medical patients had a template for living, a theory for how to be happy, and an organizing principle that coordinated activities and guided the relating to oneself and others. By following those templates, patterns, and organized lifestyle, a measure of meaning was experienced. (This is not to say that all medical patients had been happy in their premorbid life.)

After symptom onset, however, many medical patients find that those same templates and patterns are curtailed or precluded, and when that occurs the quality of their life is diminished. Yet, illness and infirmity does not have to foreclose on a satisfying existence, if patients have a willingness to find meaning in their lives. That pursuit, though, is more complicated for medical patients who are limited in many other ways. This chapter offers guidelines for medical patients for how to develop a new template for living, by combining new and old interests as modified by disease limitations.

LIFE IN TRANSITION

Disease forces many patients to enter a time of transition where flux and chaos reign. This is a precarious and frightening time, not knowing what the disease will do to the prevailing lifestyle, or in the case of terminal illness, not knowing when life will end. It is a time marked by insecurity and instability as too many aspects of lifestyle become subject to unknown conditions (e.g., the vagaries of prognosis, the fickleness of employers or significant others). "All transitions involve leaving a consolidated self behind before any new self can take its place" (Bridges, 1980, p. 232). Transitions are discontinuity before continuity can resume. While in transition, life is in limbo, existing in an in-between world—the chasm between two planes of existence, one that has ended and one that has not yet begun.

Medical patients may or may not have liked their lives before symptom onset, but it was still their own to live, with more control over outcome. With symptom onset, however, they find "that what made sense before, what held life together, what provided patterns of significance and intentionality, has broken apart thrusting these individuals into a transitional stage between the new and the old" (Carlsen, 1988, p. 3). Self-representations, life direction, and life designs that offered meaning are destroyed, altered, delayed, impeded, or detoured. Disease then pushes patients headlong into the cold, swirling waters of transition, and they do not know where those waters will carry them. Choices diminish. At the same time new templates that are not wanted and are not as satisfying must begin (e.g., seeing doctors, recuperating in bed, spending large blocks of time alone).

If disease is the current sweeping patients along, to regain some control over one's own life, to establish a lifestyle that can be satisfying, to ease the flux and chaos, meaning-making becomes crucial. Transitions do lead somewhere. Every ending does lead to a beginning that may or may not be wanted, but the form of that beginning depends on someone's willingness to create meaning. By being willing, self-control and personal power return to the individual. What the disease taketh away, *meaning-making* can give back. It allows patients to cocreate their world, along with disease and the treatment for it. It is the bridge to new templates, models, ideals, values, organization, direction, and self-representations.

Meaning-making is the continuation of individuation, the drive to express who one is (Frankl, 1965). It focuses the person on growing again, made necessary by disease. Often, individuation slows or plateaus in adult life as the set of current abilities and interests is sufficient for producing a satisfying life. Once those abilities and interests are limited, patients are forced to explore the self again to discover its potential and learn what it can offer. Individuation beckons patients to take on challenges, stretch, explore, risk, and choose what can be beneficial. It establishes a life separate from one's life as a medical patient.

FACTORS IN MEANINGFULNESS

To understand the drive to a meaningful existence, we first need to understand what has been lost due to disease. First, the life direction may no longer be motivating. The person with disease may no longer care to pursue the grand scheme that previously motivated him/her; other factors become more important, such as loss of health or possible loss of life itself. The goals that individuals worked toward for so many years suddenly appear inconsequential compared with those other issues. When this happens, purposefulness dissipates and striving to be better wanes. Accompanying that is a loss of energy to sustain the drive to attain goals. That energy is often trapped in a paralyzing depression that saps determination and resolution. In place of the previously significant goals, new goals that are mundane and stir little excitement need to be pursued, such as overcoming lethargy or pain and getting out of bed earlier in the morning. Because of the loss of physical functioning, the scope for attainment diminishes, which in turn limits choices available to the patient. With less choice, there is not as much potential for significant activities. There is also the loss of certainty and predictability. Choices for activities made in the morning may not be feasible in the afternoon, due to changes in the body. With an increase in uncertainty, the striving to find meaning can wane and is replaced by the "Why try?" philosophy.

To overcome these problems, providers need to ensure that several factors are present.

1) There needs to be a life direction, small or big, it need not matter, and it must be pursued daily. Sternbach and Rusk (1973), Sternbach (1978), and Fordyce (1976) have patients contract to meet goals. Purposefulness needs to be reinstated. Even if life is ending, terminally ill patients still need a purpose for how they will spend whatever days they have left.

2) There must be commitment, determination and resolution to attain goals. Medical patients simply have to create goals, something to get them out of bed in the morning. They have to have an aim, intentionality, and deliberateness. In part, this involves stirring interest, allocating energy, and then using it for something that has value.

3) Value has to be found, especially when so much of what has been valued has been lost due to disease or treatment. There needs

to be significant goals that the person cares about, that are pleasing, satisfying, and beneficial.

4)   There must be a means to reach the end goal. The steps to reach a goal have to be specified (Sternbach and Rusk, 1973). This involves an order and organization of self and environment that facilitates goal attainment. This also involves functionality, skill development, and role maintenance. When all of these factors work together, self-control returns. The search for meaning can ensue.

However, if providers encounter a flagging drive to find meaning, they need to shift the focus to *instilling hope,* an essential ingredient for change (Frank, 1974). Providers must reassure and sound certain that worthwhile goals and new directions can still be found and secured with ample resolution and determination. Patients do not have to be convinced that disease does not preclude a meaningful life. They just have to be curious if that is possible. The job of the therapist is to spark that curiosity.

If patients cannot feel hopeful, then the focus needs to shift to self-talk: what are they saying to themselves that makes them believe that a meaningful life is impossible. Help patients listen to their own doomsday prophecies that depletes their enthusiasm. At that point, treatment can turn to cognitive restructuring to examine beliefs that are not realistic or accurate. Meaning-making cannot proceed as long as the patient's focus is on limitation and not potential.

If curiosity can be stirred, however, if *meaning-making* can be energized, then therapy is ready to present the mechanics of how to attain meaning. The patient needs to understand that it is a skill and a technology and not just something that is stumbled upon.

ROOTS OF CREATIVITY

Meaning-making is an ability to build significant activities and pursuits. It is an act of creativity. To be able to find meaning, the roots of the creative process need to be understood. Arieti (1976) discusses several elements necessary for creativity.

1.   Aloneness: Time alone for periods of time is required to carefully hear the inner self as it makes contact with its own thoughts, emotions, and resources.
2.   Inactivity: Time away from constant motion is important to daydream, reflect, and muse about various life situations.

3. Free-thinking: A state of abandon from normal patterns, tastes, and routines is necessary. Effort has to be made to set aside preconception and overcome inhibition. Premature judgment and biases must be curtailed so they do not defuse exploration. Openness to think about whatever is encouraged. This includes thinking about opposing positions. To do this, an ability to tolerate tension between opposites is necessary. Free thinking helps to synthesize and integrate new and contrary ways of operating that can form an expanded version of self.
4. Gullibility: A willingness to be "taken in" by new activities and be absorbed by them is needed. The intent is being willing to be influenced by what is foreign, and to entertain possibilities. An innocence or naivete is important when encountering a situation, so it is experienced without the contamination of judgment, standards, and prejudice.
5. Alertness: Awareness is crucial to look for aspects of the environment that may be interesting.
6. Discipline: An ability to stay with an activity to develop competence in a skill is vital.

To create meaning, several of these elements will need to be made into skills, so the patient knows how to practice them. Five skills necessary for creativity will now be presented: 1) aloneness, 2) awareness, 3) experiencing the experience, 4) reflection, and 5) experimentation. See disc for self-evaluation form to develop these abilities.

ALONENESS TRAINING

To create meaning, medical patients need to engage in short meetings with themselves, where they reflect on what is wanted and how to achieve it. A temporary pause is required that is long enough to learn what is missing and what can be satisfying. The aloneness moment should be present-centered, focusing on who the person is at that time. One does not necessarily have to literally retreat from the scene and seek a solitary place. The aloneness moment can occur even while in motion, while engaging in an activity. What is required is a *turning into oneself* to become temporarily mentally detached from the environment. The senses that take in the world—vision, hearing, touch—become passive. At the same time the sense of the inner self is active.

AWARENESS TRAINING

Once alone with oneself, awareness is employed like a light shining on the experience. The intent is to know the experience keenly and acutely, to learn about present desires, beliefs, emotions, physical reactions, and behavioral intention. Awareness touches what one is. It informs the person about the dimensions in the situation. It illuminates potential in a context and what is wanted from it. It moves people to get what they want (Zinker, 1977).

In meaning-making, awareness actually supersedes aloneness. Patients have to become self-aware before making use of alone times. Once aware, a moment of solitude can yield much more information. If a patient lacks awareness, then the therapy task is to develop this capacity. Gestalt therapy offers many awareness exercises that heighten that function (Perls et al., 1951; Naranjo, 1980).

Awareness yields information about wants. Knowing about wants is critical. "A want is a linking function, integrating present experience with the future where its gratification lies . . . making sense out of the sensations and feelings which lead to this moment of wanting" (Polsters, 1973, p. 228). A want links the person to the objective world and is a precondition for making contact with it.

If patients are unaware of what they want, they need to be trained in how to recognize a want. They often appear in subtle ways or are unconscious. Yet, they must be revealed. For example, after Bruce's heart attack, he lay on his hospital bed wistfully looking out the window. He wanted something but was unsure of what. When he got home, he continued to look out the window as he recuperated in bed. Finally he realized what he wanted. When able, he had his wife drive him to a park where he sat for a while. He wanted a reconnection with nature during a time when he feared a loss of connection to the world. Nature also gave him a feeling of peace when his life was in flux. To know what he truly wanted, Bruce had to have an aloneness moment, where he disengaged from the world long enough to hear the quiet call within him to secure something.

Patients need to know which wants can be ignored and which must be satisfied. Some wants that are not satisfied will continue to cry out for attention. They remain as unfinished business and demand resolution. Bruce remained fascinated with the outdoors until he knew what he wanted from it. That resolved, he was then ready to entertain new wants. Here are guidelines for patients regarding wants.

1. Discover a want. *Medical patients must have wants for each day.* If none are known then create a want.

2. Clarify values. Find what is valued that day. Values will change daily. Watch the ebb and flow of wants as they advance or recede in prominence.
3. Commit to satisfying that want. Better yet, make it a public declaration so you put pressure on you to fulfill that want.
4. Scale down a want. Some wants are big or global in nature, encompassing someone's life. Examples are the need for respect, financial stability, or job security. However, big wants have to be "chunked down" to smaller pieces, where one has a small way to accomplish a big want.
5. Form a plan for accomplishing a want. For example, if you want more respect for yourself, how can you secure respect that day? Create the means to that end.
6. Put a want on a timetable. Schedule when it will be satisfied. Meaning-making is a time management affair. It must be part of an organized activity.
7. Fit a want into a block of time. For example, while waiting to see the doctor, how can you make that time more meaningful? While driving to see the doctor, what can make that time more enjoyable or memorable? This will involve the skill of *problem-solving* that will work in tandem with awareness. The latter illuminates what is wanted and the former finds avenues to get there.

EXPERIENCING THE EXPERIENCE

Once there is knowledge of the self and what is wanted from the world at a given moment, the patient rejoins the world to pursue the meaningful activity. Interacting with the environment creates an experience, but it has to be experienced with sharpened awareness to convert it into a meaningful moment (Van De Riet et al., 1980). *Experiencing the experience means feeling* one's emotions as the activity is proceeding, the effect of a belief on oneself, the effect of others on the body, and the consequences of an action. It allows someone to be taken in by the experience and moved by it. Experiences need to occur with an innocence about them, without preconception and prejudgment. This is what Husserl (1970) terms the *lebenswelt*, the here-and-now time that encapsulates the world into which the person is born, his past experiences and future yearnings. It is the intersection where being and consciousness meet.

By experiencing the experience, two types of knowledge are gained: vivid knowledge that stands out and intense knowledge that combines intellectual understanding with emotional recognition of what is. This knowledge teaches the person what is valuable, when the valued object or activity is keenly felt.

To experience the experience, patients need to be taught to *slow down the moment* to discover its dimensions. They have to be trained to stay in the here and now, to learn what they want at the moment (Perls, 1966; Naranjo, 1980). Next, they need to be taught to move among dimensions and not become stuck on one in particular. Each dimension should be processed in serial fashion, moving from one to another. So many medical patients have both positive and negative dimensions in their experiences and each has to be noted. The negative dimensions (e.g., fatigue, pain, loss of positive appearance) can too easily capture attention. The positive dimensions are often more elusive but they have to be noted to be enjoyed. For example, the slow gait of some patients due to anatomical problems can create an "impatience with self" dimension. That frustration can become foreground and dominate the experience. But at the same time, by moving slowly, more of the world can be noticed. Hence, that patient can be asked to explore slowness, by observing intricacies of situations that otherwise would be passed over.

Another skill requires a **shifting ability** to move back and forth between interacting with the world and experiencing the effect of the world on oneself. The former has been called "up-time," when people go up and into life around them, and the latter has been called "down-time," when people go down into themselves to experience the subjective world.

REFLECTION

Once someone learns the facets of their experience, there is a need to reflect on it by pausing in the activity for another aloneness moment. The action then moves into the internal sphere for reflection. Be careful of this though, because reflection cuts people off from their experience and takes them away from the here-and-now. Skill is needed to know when the experience has lasted long enough to be clearly felt, before beginning cogitation.

Reflection is an important activity for medical patients, whose activities are complicated by their condition. Contact with the world is much more involved for them. Consideration of consequences from an activity will weigh on decision-making. The moment of reflection includes such issues as past experiences in that situation, the history behind the present situation, assessment of present physical condition, and consequences that can arise from more activity. Reflection allows time to propose and answer questions such as "Can I do more? Can I be satisfied with what I have done? How will stopping now affect others?"

Problem-solving will be a primary activity during reflection. It will identify pros and cons of each activity. Some activities will have a higher cost and reward associated with it and that has to be weighed (e.g., taking a walk is invigorating but can cause increased pain). Alternative solution thinking is used to learn what else can offer meaning in that situation. Means-end thinking forms the plan and will identify tactics for getting what is wanted.

To illustrate how meaning-making will operate with the combined usage of each of these four skills, we will discuss a father with end-stage cancer who wants to improve his relationship with his teenage daughter, who is busily communicating with friends on the internet, her most preferred activity. He is aware that he doesn't have much time to live and wants to have more meaningful moments with her. He stops to experience his sadness and realizes that, being a professional, he has wasted many opportunities for pursuing a closer relationship with his child. This experience increases the poignancy of the need to make contact with her. In an aloneness moment, he becomes aware of his fondness for her, and his need to take care of her. By experiencing his experience, his daughter stands out more vividly in his mind and his love for her increases in intensity. He learns what he wants: a verbal exchange with her. He then shifts to reflect on his past history of contacts with her when she was on the computer, and her difficulty dealing with his impending death. He notes that she usually responds with irritation whenever others seek her attention while she is on the computer. He is aware that she refuses to talk about his dying. Alternative solution thinking informs him about gradients of meaningful activities that he can pursue with her. He elects a level of contact that does not challenge her but offers a chance for a satisfying interchange: asking her how she is doing, telling her that he loves her, and asking her if she wants anything to drink. By reflecting on past history, he knows that this approach will reduce the possibility of an unpleasant moment, which he wants to avoid. He then approaches her, has a quick but pleasant exchange about nothing important, and takes her order for what she wants to drink. He then experiences the dimension of being her caretaker, which feels meaningful to him. While this is an inconsequential activity, it stands out in his mind. He has made a moment of meaning.

EXPERIMENTATION

In general, medical patients have choices regarding what can be meaningful to them. They can seek to overcome the losses stemming from their disease. They can tenaciously focus on resurrection of past patterns and roles compromised or terminated by the disease or treatment. Certainly that may be needed if security and stability rest on them. At the same time they can also move in another direction that seriously looks at who they are, what is wanted, and what they can become. In this regard patients are viewing their illness not only as a curse but perhaps a blessing for giving them an opportunity to be different than they were.

To gain this opportunity, medical patients need to venture into the role of experimenter (Osborn, 1963). This involves free thinking and gullibility, two of the components of creativity already discussed. Experimentation is a willingness to vary oneself, lifestyle, relationships, patterns, self-representations and roles, and then assess the outcome. If the results are deemed desirable, then the experiment alters normal life operating to include more of the new way of being. At the heart of experimentation are two qualities. One is the spirit to be adventure-some—"let's see what will happen." The second is a willingness to be a scientist, to hatch an idea that something can be significant, to test if the idea is correct, and then assess the results. Providers need to encourage these two qualities.

Experimentation is a crucial activity for medical patients. As the disease is better understood, patients learn how they can function with their symptoms and condition, and how much function will be lost. They are then able to experiment with other ways to find meaning besides their traditional patterns of being. Doing so, they realize that patterns in the premorbid state are only one way the self can proceed in life. Dabbling in possibility, they find other versions of self become possible. Existentialists (Maslow, 1954) refer to this activity as self-actualization: becoming who one is.

Gestalt, though, fears self-actualization will be blocked by character (Perls, 1972), which creates a rigidity of self that only allows for the expression of a set version of the individual. Hence, character would circumscribe meaning-making, demand pattern fixity, and resist experimentation. By its very nature, character seeks the status quo and wants to change very little, preferring more of the same. Oppositely, experimentation wants to see what can happen next, and seeks a fluid, changing self that evolves over time.

So many medical patients miss the opportunity to experiment, when they stay focused on returning to the image they had of themselves in the premorbid state. They have a set concept of what the self should be and little variance from that image is allowed. Self-love is felt when they come closest to realizing that concept. Perls (1972) has referred to this as self-image actualization, and he maintains that it moves in opposition to self-actualization. Self-image actualization is what leads to character. It gives people pride and raises self-esteem through role fulfillment and pattern maintenance. Disease, though, threatens self-image actualization by preventing role maintenance.

While Perls saw self-image actualization and self-actualization as competing urges, CCT does not. CCT believes that each has a place in the life of a patient, and that therapy should support both. In regard to supporting self-image actualization, patients can be encouraged to seek abridged role maintenance, if their condition precludes full role participation. This means fulfilling a scaled-down version of old roles for periods of the day, such as part-time jobs or part-time volunteer work. Two cases serve as examples. Ruth, a long-term care patient, was encouraged to make outreach calls for a community theater seeking volunteers (e.g., discussing upcoming events, asking for contributions). Darnell, a long-term care patient who can do little physically, was encouraged to become a student at an on-line university.

In regard to self-actualization, patients are encouraged to explore who they are and seek to fulfill dormant or discouraged interests. Ned, an HIV positive patient, had to decide about going back to accounting, a steady, good-paying job that his parents wanted him to continue (self-image actualization), or pursue more creative ways to earn a living that tapped into other facets of himself. Brainstorming with his therapist, he chose to give up accounting and instead become a specialist in artistic wall painting.

Frequently patients do not know where experimentation will lead them, compared with self-image actualization, a known entity. Substantial reassurance is needed to stimulate patients to venture into the unknown, when old patterns are no longer possible due to the disease. Daryl, an MS patient, lost his ability to be a biker, his beloved avocation that circumscribed how he dressed and acted. A vacuum developed in his life. Asking him what he liked to watch on TV, Daryl said that he enjoyed the nature channel a lot. The therapist inquired if he would be interested in zoology. That did not fit into Daryl's image of a rough and tumble biker, though. Self-image actualization was blocking self-actualization. To overcome this problem, the therapist prodded him to read zoology texts and he found them fascinating. With even more prodding, he began taking college courses in that subject.

As medical patients find new ways to express themselves and new interests to pursue, a moment of recognition is needed to appreciate what they have. That is the time for thankfulness. It acts to highlight and savor whatever is meaningful.

THANKFULNESS TRAINING

In the crisis phase, chronic and terminal illness patients find very little to be thankful for. There are multiple losses and changes for the worse. Complaints fill the mind and are voiced freely. An overall disgruntled feeling overhangs experiences, as patients feel discontented.

In the consolidation phase this changes considerably, as patients adjust to their disease. The body may not be liked but there is more of an ability to accommodate to changes. Meaning-making has given patients new interests. There is much less bitterness. At this point medical patients are ready to appreciate what they *have* instead of focusing on what they have lost. This means expressing thankfulness for what life has brought.

Encouraging chronic and terminally ill patients to be thankful may seem strange when they appear to have so little to be thankful for. Yet, it offers several benefits. It finds positive parts to a life and positions them into the foreground of the mind. When that occurs, disease drifts into the background, allowing matters other than health-related concerns to come to the fore. Life is then celebrated instead of being damned, which in turn diminishes bitterness and replaces it with the joy of receiving. This facilitates the transition from feeling troubled and discontented to satisfied. Enjoyment of life may also lead to a spiritual reawakening. During the crisis phase, many patients became alienated from religion due to anger with God for not curing them. Thankfulness, though, may reunite patients with God.

Many patients will have to practice a set of subskills to gain an appreciative, grateful response, because it will not come naturally for them. When symptoms first arise, there is little focus on positive elements in life. Happy events may still occur but they receive much less notice. *Awareness* will then be needed to allow patients to appreciate those times. Next, they will need to participate in *crediting*. This involves giving credit to who or what deserves recognition for delivering a benefit. Others' contributions are acknowledged. A moment is taken to feel appreciation. This leads to the skill of *savoring*, a perceptual-emotional ability, where an object is held in foreground, viewed intently, and at the same time is experienced. To make crediting a routine activity, thanking sessions may need to be scheduled each day, at meals or before bedtime. If patients have difficulty finding the good in their lives, *objectivity training* can be used. In this practice, the patient is asked to see their situation from a distance or as someone else. Viewing their life from a distance, the good can be seen more clearly mixed in with the bad.

Summary

As medical patients become used to having an illness, they need to form new patterns that can develop into a satisfying existence. That is part of the task of meaning-making. It considers old interests while integrating the limitations of pursuing them. From this a synthesis is formed that combines old ways with new ways. Meaning-making requires several abilities including solitude to learn about one's interests, self-awareness, experiencing the experience to know if a pursuit is satisfying, and reflection about when and how to continue that activity. There is a need for experimentation to find new ways to be happy. There will be many times when medical patients are happy and they need to feel thankful at those moments. That will increase appreciation for what they have, that which enriches their lives.

Limitation Management

I know I have made progress, but sometimes I fall into a depression thinking about my old self. I cannot do a lot. I get upset when I realize that.

—Brenda, MS patient

In the previous chapter, the issue of meaning-making was discussed. However, this important activity will not be successful if medical patients cannot come to terms with their own limitations. They will not seek new or different ways to find meaning if they are routinely sidetracked about being helpless and deprived. They will not feel excited about forming a new life if they are constantly consumed with regret, remorse, and frustration about not having the life they once had.

Disease does impose limitations on people in numerous ways. Dislike of being restricted will arise throughout the medical condition. Being able to manage such restrictions will determine how well patients grow accustomed to their disease, and how much they adjust to the loss of their health. Thus, dealing with limitation becomes a dominant task of medical patients.

This chapter discusses two aspects of that task: *limitation integration* and *limitation maintenance*. The former skill is used when patients seek to live with the restrictions imposed by their disease. This is vital to avoid a backlash against their condition. The latter skill is practiced to curb other people's interference with meaning-making activities, so patients are able to develop the life they want.

LIMITATION INTEGRATION

Limitation is experienced in two different ways. When blocked from getting one's way, and that blockage cannot be overcome, a feeling of helplessness arises. Being restricted prevents patients from getting what they want, which creates a feeling of deprivation. This section of the chapter discusses how to cope with each of these feelings and focuses on how to respond when limitation cannot be side stepped or eradicated.

HELPLESSNESS TOLERANCE

Helplessness occurs when someone lacks internal or external means to attain a goal. There is an inability to manage by oneself, and at the same time others cannot remedy the problem, leaving a person feeling powerless and lacking self-efficacy. Helplessness is the experience of floundering, impotency, and ineffectuality. While acceptance means recognizing reality, helplessness means someone recognizes the fact that there are no behavioral means to change reality and attain the desired outcome. This does not mean the quest has to be abandoned, but there is the knowledge that no solution to a problem or means to the end is available.

Medical patients routinely encounter helplessness when they butt against their physical limitations. It is felt when the body will not cooperate: limbs will not move, energy is lacking, or tissue aches too much to accomplish a task. Physical inability literally means helplessness, where capacity is weakened or destroyed.

While no one likes being ineffectual, there are factors that make ineffectiveness even harder to tolerate. One factor is background, where there is extensive prior experience with being defenseless and unprotected against a harsh, superior force, so when helplessness is encountered again as part of the disease experience it feels overwhelming. A second factor may have been a past trauma in a patient's life. Helplessness is one of the basic elements of trauma, so when the former is experienced as part of a medical condition, the latter is reexperienced at the same time. A third factor is when there has been a series of recent situations where someone has lost control over his or her life. Then, when helplessness is experienced as part of the disease experience it becomes too much to bear. In essence, the *ability to absorb* any more powerlessness has been "maxed out," and depression ensues (Abramson et al., 1989).

Thoughts about the helpless situation can create problems, such as the absolutistic thought, "I cannot stand not having control in this situation. It must not be this way." The belief places a demand on oneself to find a way to attain the elusive goal. If no way can be found, a further thought complicates the situation even more, "Being helpless is awful."

A final factor is personality itself. Some patients have an agonistic personality, where they habitually fight against any force limiting them in any way. They have a personality that struggles to get their way; surrender is very difficult for them. Hence, when they encounter limitations imposed by disease or treatment, frustration is greater because they hate to be limited or lose to any overpowering force. Their natural or learned tendency is to continue to wage a battle to overcome restriction.

The agonistic tendency is not in and of itself problematic. It pays major dividends in some situations such as cancer where the fight to stay alive is crucial. On the other hand it exacerbates some stressful situations by pushing the self to battle on when little can be gained. Greater resentment is then felt when victory remains elusive.

As part of assessment, providers need to inquire why the ineffectual condition is so frustrating for some patients. Has being held back or kept down always been a problem for that patient? Are there times when a patient can accept being squelched or restricted better than other times, and why is that? Next, providers need to inquire how much frustration is felt when someone feels helpless. Secure a quantitative rating, from zero to five, with five standing for fury about being restricted. (See disc*** for self-evaluation questionnaire to assess response to helplessness.)

This will lead into the induction for *helplessness tolerance*: "Are you interested in being *less* upset and frustrated when you are limited in some way?" If the answer is affirmative, then the skill is presented as an ability to *endure impotency* and a lack of power and control.

When presenting this skill, define it as an internal activity and not a behavioral position regarding surrendering or not surrendering to situational limitation. In actuality, helplessness tolerance does not preclude seeking to change the course of the situation. One can still fight to overcome restriction while at the same time practice helplessness tolerance when his or her efforts have not met with success.

Here are the executive beliefs patients say to themselves to develop this ability:

1. Tolerate being powerless in this situation. Increase forbearance when the means to the end is blocked, e.g., "Put up with not getting what I want. I can handle it."
2. Work to soothe anger and frustration about not getting my way. Practice frustration tolerance. To manage anger, practice such

skills as *relaxation* to stay calm, *sensory diversion* to get my mind off of what's upsetting me, and self-instructions, e.g., "Don't get upset. I can't always get my way."

3. Shun self-pity about being limited. Don't get into "poor me."
4. Do not make a fuss about not getting my way. Stop protesting a lack of control. That will only make me more angry.
5. Forge a realistic position about being hindered or stinted (e.g., "I cannot always get what I want. It is desirable to get my way, but that is not always possible. Accept that fact. Limitations exist. They come with my condition. Deal with them.").
6. Do not demand control in a situation where there is little ability to exercise it. I can still continue to wish for power while I may not have it.
7. View futility and incapacity to attain goals not as awful, merely as undesirable. Rationally look at being checked as unfortunate but not terrible.
8. Accept the fact that at this moment I am helpless. Integrate this condition into my life, so it is part of my existence (e.g., "I cannot get what I want so I must live with it. Being powerless is now part of my life.")
9. Decide if the struggle to get my way will be continued. If so, establish reasonable goals for what can be changed. Use *area thinking* in this regard. Push only for goals that are within my area of influence.

If these points are put into a self-instruction dialogue, then there must be sentences to prepare the patient for a situation where s/he may not be able to get what is wanted to avoid a descent into self-pity or anger. There must also be sentences to assuage anger and frustration when there is a lack of control (see disc*** for self-dialogue).

If consternation remains about being helpless, symbolic gesturing can be used as a response substitution tactic, employed when there is excessive anger and protest about being helpless. For example, when frustration is felt, the patient can extend his/her forearm and pretend to be grasping something strongly. Have the hand shake with tension at that time. This symbolizes a strong, continued effort to get one's way. Then, as part of the push to decline battling against helplessness, have the hand and arm go limp. That symbolizes acceptance of inability to accomplish one's intent, and willingness to bear that fact.

To make the point that helplessness can be tolerated, solution-oriented therapy can be used (de Shazer, 1985, 1988, 1991; Berg and Miller, 1992). Patients monitor moments during the week when they are helpless but that does not cause chagrin or protest. Next, they identify what they are thinking and doing at that time to facilitate tolerance of helplessness. Those coping responses are then assigned to other situations.

Some patients, though, will not reveal coping responses to restriction. They have a most difficult time adjusting when they are ineffectual or powerless. In part, that is because they cling to a strategy of rejecting helplessness instead of coexisting with it. In that case, a paradoxical approach can be used, by giving permission and even encouraging the behavioral struggle to gain what is wanted (even though the effort will not be rewarded). At the same time stress the internal response to not getting one's way. Therapist: "By all means, don't let me stop you from pushing to get what you want, even though doing so will cost you in several ways, or offer meager results. The main issue is how upset will you be when your efforts are not met with success?" This approach indirectly encourages patients to do something that will be self-injurious, which may foment defiance against the prescription. It also points the patient in the desired direction: tolerating being helpless when it cannot be avoided. It does not try to change the absolutistic policy belief "I must not be helpless." It allows those who choose to overcome their helpless situation (a behavioral activity) to continue to do so, but as long as they work on helplessness tolerance (an internal activity) they will have *livable* negative emotions from taking a nonsurrender strategy.

If they choose to fight against their helpless situation, and that is causing difficulties, that will have to be addressed as well. Some behavioral strategies are irrational and nonutilitarian. Cognitive restructuring is helpful for treating that problem. It can realistically assess the wisdom of pursuing a nonsurrender strategy. It addresses the irrational demands the patient places on himself to battle on when helplessness cannot be avoided. It changes the driven nature of agonistic striving, by giving patients a reasonable way to think about their situation: "I would like not to be helpless. That would be preferable. It is not a must that I attain my goals, but it is desirable if I do." Thinking in terms of desire reduces the all-out push to gain control in situations offering only minimal control.

Another cognitive restructuring tactic can help patients realize when a nonsurrender strategy is unrealistic and unwise. After they state their absolutistic demand about not being helpless, the therapist gives the realistic conditions for satisfying that demand. Therapist: "So what I hear you say is, 'I must find a way to clean the house before the kids get home, even though my body is quite fatigued and weak and cannot go on. I must find a way to overcome this fatigue even though I haven't figured out a way in the past.' Is this what you are saying?" This is a forced encountering of reality, which may alter the command to overcome physical limitations. (Bear in mind, though, that even if patients feel less driven to overcome their powerlessness, they will still need to practice helplessness tolerance. They will still feel frustration over not getting their way and that has to be tolerated.)

We now turn our attention to what will be felt when patients remain helpless and cannot get what they want. That is the feeling of deprivation.

DEPRIVATION ALLOWANCE

Deprivation is felt when something is taken away from a person or a person cannot attain his/her goals. A vacuum exists in that case; a want or need remains, creating an incomplete or unfinished feeling. Deprivation also occurs when a "possession" is lost and cannot be regained. For chronic or terminally ill patients, the "possession" is one's life, mobile legs, strong muscles, an energetic body, respect from a spouse, or financial security. The loss of these "possessions" occurs daily and cannot be avoided because they are facets or prototypical features of the disease. Deprivation, in that case, comes with having a disease, which means medical patients will need to practice the skill of *deprivation tolerance* to avoid the frustration and anger from not satisfying one's need. See disc for self-dialogue to attain this ability.***

There are some patients, though, who will refuse to practice that skill. They adjust poorly to deprivation and cannot bear a shortage, loss, and forfeiture of what they care about. They resist and battle on to get want they want. They, too, have an agonistic tendency and engage in absolutistic thinking: "This (dissatisfaction, sacrifice, depletion) should not be happening to me. I should have what I want. Life's not fair. It's not right."

This group of patients will need the skill of *deprivation allowance*. This skill works to stop the irrational internal battle against deprivation by allowing it to exist when it cannot be avoided. It organizes a cognitive-affective-physiological response to live with reality, when privation is mandated by the medical condition. It urges patients to stop rejecting, hating, and damning circumstances (e.g., disease, treatment side effects, significant others) that forces deprivation on them. It seeks adjusting to the reality that disease is costly. While acknowledging no one wants to suffer shortage and wantage when it cannot be avoided, it allows people to make room for it.

CCT addresses the matter of deprivation similarly to how it addresses helplessness. It often does not counter the behavioral strategy to struggle to obtain what is wanted, if that is the chosen course. In fact, CCT may even encourage the agonistic tendency on a behavioral level, to develop tenacity and perseverance. Patients are told, "Do what you can behaviorally to limit sacrifice of what you care about." At the same time, CCT wants cessation of the internal battle against deprivation, which is manifested as brooding, discontent, complaining, and self-pity.

For example, Beth, a chronically fatigued patient, is encouraged to battle against her tendency to give in to her fatigue. She is asked to do more for herself to satisfy her needs. Her therapist encourages an agonistic tendency when it is helpful. He encourages thinking in terms of *should* when its appropriate. At the same time, when a deficiency of satisfaction cannot be avoided, she is asked to allow deprivation into her life.

One way to develop deprivation tolerance is by creating a self-instruction dialogue that forges a substitute response when patients slip into rejecting deprivation internally. Here is an example of a self-dialogue written for William, a dying cancer patient in his early thirties and father of two young children. Constructive mourning was first tried to help him express his fury that he will be deprived of experiences other men his age will enjoy. He continued being bitter, though. When he thought of dying, rancor filled his body. Yet, he did not want to die feeling angry and bitter, although he was not able to overcome his resentment that immediately erupted when he thought about his many losses. Working conjointly with his therapist, the following self-dialogue was implemented and repeated whenever bitterness was felt about deprivation.

Self-Statements Before Seeing My Children

They will be coming home from school soon. Don't fall into resentment and bitterness when seeing them. I won't be filled with anger about not being part of their lives because I will die soon.

Let the anger go. Let the situation be, because I cannot change it, although I dislike it thoroughly.

Enjoy the time with them. Fill my life with pleasure—not hatred.

Don't hold grudges against God or fortune for taking away my life.

Self-Statements When Feeling Bitter About Dying

Watch out for my musts, like 'This must not happen to me. I must not die and leave my children. I must live to see them grow up.'

Those musts will only make me sadder. I cannot meet these musts.

I do not want to die but those are "the cards" dealt to me. Accept the cards I have been dealt. They are not what I want, but I have no other hand to play.

Try to live on as long as I can and live each day fully without bitterness.

When repeated several times a day, the dialogue did gradually help William change his mindless, emotionally driven response to death. It helped him address the limitations imposed by death. He was gradually able to integrate those limitations into his life.

To further inculcate the response to accept limitation, William's therapist also utilized symbolic gesturing. He had William say the phrase, "No, I refuse to accept" while pushing against the air in front of him. That movement symbolized trying to push away privation. Then, he took in a deep breath and brought his hands slowly toward his chest, to symbolize letting deprivation come closer to him. Finally, when he said the phrase, "It will happen," he let his hands touch his chest, and at that point deprivation was allowed to literally touch his life.

Some patients may have difficulty employing a self-instruction training format or cognitive restructuring, because they have such extensive anger and grief about their losses. In that case *constructive mourning* may need to be used prior to engaging in cognitive-oriented treatments, to ease sorrow about a depleted life.

LIMITATION MAINTENANCE

The above discussion views limitation as realization of an inability to achieve a desired outcome. There are other ways to view limitation, such as restricting other's involvement, or limiting other's effect or influence. In this regard limitation is something that needs to be maintained, to preserve the patient's choice or basic essence. It is a fence that prevents incursions by others who want to gain access into the patient's mental and/or physical space. It is something that maintains a personal agenda, prerogatives, purpose, and commitment.

SELF-TUNING

Limitation on others becomes necessary once meaning-making has succeeded in broadening the medical patient's life, having given back what disease had taken away. At that point, the challenge is preserving what has been developed. Once a course of action has been decided upon, the next task is avoiding being co-opted by other people's agendas.

To maintain an individual course, a skill is needed: *self-tuning* (Sharoff, 2002). It operates the same as tuning a radio into a desired station. One station is tuned in and that is the "self-station." Other stations—other people's agendas—are tuned out momentarily. Hence, self-tuning has a dual function. It blocks other people's influence and allows patients to stay focused on what they care about, thus facilitating the individuation process.

Self-tuning facilitates patient integrity. It is practiced to avoid turning the medical patient into a sheep who blindly follows what the health provider or significant other demands of him. It seeks to put patients in charge of their lives and medical programs. It is not a call for selfishness or ignoring the rest of the world. It does not promote self-absorption. Other people's needs must also be considered. The decision to please others has to be carefully weighed against what is then best for the patient.

The need for self-tuning often comes about not just because others are self-centered and only want the patient to please them. It is often needed because family, friends, or health care providers are loving and care about what is best for the patient. In their zeal to show caring they may try to take over the patient's life, wholeheartedly believing that they know best.

Sometimes they do know best; sometimes their point is correct. In order to know when it is advisable to heed another person's message, *objectivity* is required. This skill requires patients to pull back mentally from their own position for the moment and dispassionately assess another person's position. Then, the intellect calmly weighs what the other person has to say. To make the best decision, self-tuning requires *information gathering*. It asks patients to ask questions, read about their disease, and acquire information firsthand by talking to other patients. It utilizes the ideas of others without turning them into superiors who will control their options. Then, with enough data, a decision is made and self-tuning preserves that course.

The Self-Tuning Function

Self-tuning acts in two different ways. It works to nurture new interests after the disease process has precluded premorbid pursuits. It works hand-in-hand with meaning-making and self-boosting to foster interests.

Once an interest has been considered, it works with self-boosting to promote the belief "I can do that" against the dubious, pessimistic self beaten down by the disease and treatment side effects. As self-boosting builds self-confidence that an interest can be developed, self-tuning works to sustain that interest against any incursions by others who doubt that the limited patient can take on that activity. At the same time self-tuning works to reinvigorate old interests that can still be pursued. Again, self-boosting acts as a cheerleader to encourage and motivate reinvolvement in past pursuits, and self-tuning keeps the patient focused on synthesizing a lifestyle based on old and new interests.

Some functions of self-tuning are:

- It has a policy-making function, to form plans for the self. This involves prioritizing what is best for the patient and what is best for others, and then deciding if the patient can meet other people's needs.
- It has an implementation capacity, to motivate the self to carry out the plans that have been made.
- It works hand in hand with the exoneration skill. When the patient feels inappropriate guilt about not meeting another person's needs, the exoneration protocol is employed to remove guilt.
- It creates boundaries or limitations on oneself not to take on more than he or she is capable of doing. It also places boundaries on others regarding their participation with the patient. This is part of the gatekeeper function (Fennell, 2001).
- Another gatekeeper function is ensuring a proper allocation of energy to various projects. The internal energy auditor assesses how much energy will be needed for various activities considering the patient's available energy level. Then, a decision is made whether there is sufficient energy to meet that project.
- It places patients in charge of their own treatment, so they are not pushed into doing what they do not want. By assuming a *watch guard* function, patients—not the health provider or family—decide what is best. Others may be a consultant but not the final decision maker.
- It coordinates the input of others. It places the patient in charge of the team that is involved in his/her medical program.

To illustrate the self-tuning process, we will consider the case of Michelle, a cancer patient undergoing chemotherapy.

She wanted to prove to her husband that she was still her old self. She tried to take on more than she could handle and would tire herself out. She was practicing a normalization strategy, to prove to others and herself that the cancer had not changed her as a mother and wife. Solitude helped her to realize that she really had become different physically for her body had changed due to the chemotherapy and surgery. Influenced by self-tuning, she carefully weighed others' requests and decided not to satisfy some of them. She told her boss that she was not ready to come back to work at that time. To avoid fatigue she used experimentation *to decide on other ways to please her family.*

Several months passed and Michelle had returned to her old life. Her doctor then informed her that the cancer had returned. She let the doctor take the lead and he scheduled surgery for her followed by another round of chemotherapy. After several more months, the doctor informed her that the cancer had spread. While he told her that her chances were not good, he wanted to try to remove the tumors. This time Michelle said "no, thank you" to him. She was feeling better and wanted to enjoy the last few months of her life. She knew that the chemotherapy would spoil the enjoyment of whatever time she had left. Her husband, children, and doctor opposed her plan but she used self-tuning to weigh her options and take charge of her own life.

SUBSKILLS OF SELF-TUNING

Some people will find self-tuning difficult to do. There are people pleasers who have spent their lives doing for others. There are approval seekers who want approbation above everything else. There are those who are easily susceptible to guilt. They feel badly that their illness has burdened loved ones. Each of these individuals will compensate those close to them by meeting their needs first. To treat these groups of people, providers need to inquire what they want most of all—self-control or making others happy by giving them what they want. Providers need to force patients to realize that their choices may limit their own lives.

Some will say that they want self-direction but feel conflicted when they displease others. Some have little experience sticking to their own agendas. These people will have to be trained in how to be self-tuning. They will need the following subskills.

To help patients know what they want, **values clarification** is required to determine what is most importance to the individual and what is most important to the significant others in the patient's life. The act of valuing is done on a continuum, from high to low. The end product of values clarification is a priority list of the highest valued activities or pursuits.

If medical patients elect to pursue a priority of their own, they need to engage in *energy auditing* to decide if their energy reserves are equal to accomplish that task. Healthy people by and large do not have to consider that issue, especially not on a regular basis, but the infirm do.

The energy audit will work in conjunction with another cognitive skill: *cost-benefit analysis*. It is conducted by considering several factors for and against an activity. To do an analysis, those factors can be placed on a chart. In the first column is the valued activity. In the second column is the cost to patients if they commit to a task, taking into consideration the energy needed to complete the project, present level of fatigue or pain, and possible worsening of symptoms if the action is undertaken. In the third column is the benefit to patients. The benefit and cost to patients should be a number computed on a scale from zero to five, with five being maximum benefit and maximum cost to self. A fourth column might be the cost/benefit computation to others.

After computing these various matters, a more informed decision can be made if that action should be undertaken. The ideal situation is a cost/benefit ratio where there is high benefit and low cost to the patient (e.g., 5/1). If there is high benefit but also high cost to the patient (e.g., 5/4), then that activity should be weighed carefully before an obligation is made. Likewise, if there is low benefit to self and high cost to others (e.g., 2/4) when an action is undertaken (e.g., shunning sex with a spouse), then that activity will also need to be carefully considered, because it can harm a relationship. The analysis will help patients consider the pros and cons before making a decision, so it slows down decision making, which is important if the patient is impulsive.

Once patients commit to following their own course, they realize that others may not like it. At this point two different skills are needed: *rejection tolerance* and *exoneration training*. A patient's effort to preserve self-control may seem like contrariness to others. In turn they may become rejecting. To withstand disapproval, the skill of rejection tolerance is practiced. At the same time displeasing others may cause guilt. Secure from patients an estimate of their susceptibility to feeling guilty. Logically, there will be mild guilt when displeasing a loved one, but if moderate to severe guilt is felt, then exoneration training needs to be utilized. Unless guilt is managed, medical patients may abandon personal choice and make unwise decisions just to please others.

Another way to overcome guilt is by increasing sensitivity to one's own needs, which is developed by *entitlement thinking*. This way of thinking is especially necessary for people pleasers. Entitlement thinking will operate as a cognitive-motivational activity that declares and concretizes a sense of right. It grants freedom to the patient to follow personal pursuits and makes an assertion of being deserving. If others do not agree or obstruct that endeavor, entitlement thinking pushes patients to protest others' behavior.

Sometimes there is guilt about displeasing others due to unrealistic thinking. Patients may believe they will cause others significant problems when that is not the case. At this point the skill of **consequential thinking** is used to expose unrealistic thinking, especially catastrophic thoughts. If problems for others are identified, then **alternative solution thinking** can be utilized to find the best solution for that problem. It will also be used to generate ways to satisfy significant others if the patient cannot satisfy them in the present situation.

In doing this exercise, a patient also has to ask if the original assertion of displeasing others is realistic ("Is it true that my husband will be displeased if I do that?"). That will require the use of **reality detection**, to assess if their thinking is correct. Following cognitive restructuring procedure, have patients convert their belief of displeasing others into a hypothesis and test the belief by collecting data.

If patients are determined to follow through on what they want for themselves, then interpersonal skills will be necessary. One important ability is **integrative negotiating** (Fisher, 1991). It invites all parties in a conflict to try and find ways to accommodate each other and meet everyone's needs to some extent. The goal is to please everyone in some way and urges individuals not to hold to their original position but instead make the other person's needs a focus as well as their own. Then, with all parties seeking to satisfy everyone's agendas, the focus turns to **problem-solving** to find ways to do that (Shure, 1981).

Once patients decide on following their own course, to gain what is wanted from others or to avoid incursions by others, the skill of **assertiveness** is quite important. In particular, rejection assertiveness (Kelly, 1982) needs to be learned and practiced. Passive or aggressive behavior is shunned in favor of communication that limits the chance of offending others while optimizing self-control.

IMPERVIOUSNESS TRAINING

If a patient chooses to pursue a course that others find objectionable, another skill is necessary. Patients will need **imperviousness training** if they are prone to put others first, as in the case of dependent personalities, or when there is fear of losing the approval and love of another person. Imperviousness is a type of positive brainwashing. The patient creates a mind-set that bucks the influence of another person when appropriate (Sharoff, 2002).

This requires the subskill of *insensitivity*, the ability not to feel other people's emotions, especially their pain, and not identify with their dilemma. In order to be insensitive, perspective taking needs to be avoided, by not putting oneself in another person's shoes. At the same time only one's own needs and agenda are considered.

Self-instruction training is used to create the impervious mind-set. There needs to be self-talk before and during interactions with others, to avoid being influenced by the other person. See disc for copy of dialogue.***

Self-Talk Before Dealing with Another Person

Am I prone to give in to this person? Do I hesitate to be assertive with him/her?

How important is this action to me? Clarify its importance.

How much flak will I get if I don't do what this person wants?

Weigh the costs and benefits to myself.

I really want to do this. Stick to my guns with him/her.

This is my priority. I am important, too. I have a right to be pleased.

Don't get involved with their agenda. Focus on my own.

If they get upset, don't feel their pain. Focus on what I want and my pain from not getting my way.

Self-Talk When Dealing with the Other Person

I don't have to please them all the time.

Think of what's important to me. Keep my values in the foreground.

Protect my interests. Remember I am entitled. I have a right to say "no" some of the time.

I am an independent human being and not under their control.

I am no less a person just because they are frustrated with me for not pleasing them. I still have the right to please myself.

Just because I have a disease and I disappoint others because I can't do what they want, that does not mean I owe them.

I am not obligated to pay others back because I have disappointed them in the past.

Many patients will be hesitant to practice imperviousness and insensitivity because those skills seem selfish. Reassure them that if they are sensitive, they will not suddenly ignore the needs and rights of others. These skills are not practiced as a lifestyle or general way of operating. They are only practiced selectively and situationally when there is a need for them. They are a way to maintain self-assertion in a given context when an action needs to be taken. They preserve patient rights when they are appropriate. They only reduce the excessive influence of other people.

Imperviousness training is also most important for medical patients who appear different from others due to their physical condition. These patients need to be able to proceed with their lives and not be overly sensitive to other people's stares, shock, and other negative responses. Imperviousness acts as blinders on a horse, to not "see" others when needed. Imperviousness is also helpful for not being so concerned with other's criticism for not meeting their role expectations. It allows patients to live within themselves more peacefully, by not feeling other people's anger.

CONFLUENCE TRAINING

The discussion about self-tuning, imperviousness, insensitivity, and entitlement thinking should not give the impression that this book encourages medical patients to be self-absorbed and not care for others. In contrast, it encourages balancing the care of self and care of others. At times medical patients need to consider when it is best to please others to preserve the relationship.

There are medical patients who hardly need limitation maintenance skills. They already possess those abilities. They may have been self-centered before they ever became ill, or perhaps began to put themselves first after they became ill, as a reaction to the many losses they have had to endure. If someone is too focused on themselves, then they need *confluence training*. This is an ability to flow with another person and accommodate them. Self-talk should be developed for them to control the excessive tendency to be independent and not work with other people. Part of confluence training also involves *consequential thinking*, to consider the long-range consequences of always pushing to get what is wanted, when it costs the relationship.

Summary

The dominant goal in treating chronic and terminally ill patients is helping them find peace of mind. This is accomplished by coming to terms with their limitations, by accepting them into their lives. In part this requires an ability to cope with helplessness, which occurs when someone cannot attain a goal. The skill of helplessness tolerance is required to bear the frustration of being helpless. Medical patients will be deprived in many ways and deprivation must be allowed into their lives when it cannot be avoided.

At the same time, medical patients want to pursue meaningful lives, which may put them in conflict with others. Hence, there is a need to maintain limitations on others when they seek to countermand the patient's self-control. One skill that can help in this regard is self-tuning, which keeps patients focused on their own agenda. Another skill is imperviousness, which helps patients ignore other people's agendas.

References

Abramson, L., Metalsky, G., & Alloy, L. (1989). Hopelessness depression: A theory-based subtype of depression. *Psychological Review, 96,* 358–372.

Abramson, L., Seligman, M., & Teasdale, J. (1978). Learned helplessness in humans: Critique and reformulation. *Journal of Abnormal Psychology, 87,* 49–74.

Ader, R., & Cohen, N. (1984). Behavior and the immune system. In W. D. Gentry (Ed.), *Handbook of behavioral medicine* (pp. 117–173). New York: Guilford Press.

Alberti, R., & Emmons, M. (1978). *Your perfect right: A guide to assertive behavior.* San Luis Obispo, CA: Impact Publications.

Arieti, S. (1976). *Creativity: The magic synthesis.* New York: Basic Books.

Bandler, R., & Grinder, J. (1975). *Patterns of the hypnotic techniques of Milton Erickson, M.D.* (Vol. 1). Cupertino, CA: Meta Publications.

Bandler, R., & Grinder, J. (1982). *Reframing.* Moag, UT: Real People Press.

Bandura, A. (1969). *Principles of behavior modification.* New York: Holt, Rinehart, and Winston.

Bandura, A. (1977). Self-efficacy: Toward a unifying theory of behavioral change. *Psychological Review, 84,* 191–215.

Bandura, A. (1982). Self-efficacy mechanism in human agency. *American Psychologist, 37,* 122–147.

Bandura, A. (1984). Recycling misconceptions of perceived self-efficacy. *Cognitive Therapy and Research, 8,* 231–255.

Bandura, A. (1986). *Social foundations of thought and action: A social cognitive theory.* Englewood Cliffs, NJ: Prentice-Hall.

Bandura, A. (1997). *Self-efficacy: The exercise of control.* New York: Freeman.

Barber, T. (1977). Cognitive strategies and cognitive style: Some behavioral implications. Paper presented at the annual meeting of the American Psychological Association. San Francisco. August.

Barkovec, T., Wilkinson, L., Folensbee, R., & Lerman, C. (1983). Stimulus control application to the treatment of worry. *Behavior, Research, and Therapy, 21,* 247–251.

Barlow, D. (1988). *Anxiety and its disorders: the nature and treatment of anxiety and panic.* New York: Guilford Press.

Barlow, D., Blanchard, E., Vermilyea, J., Vermilyea, B., & DiNardo, P. (1986). Generalized anxiety and generalized anxiety disorder: Description and reconceptualization. *American Journal of Psychiatry, 143,* 40–44.

Barlow, D., diNardo, P., Vermilyea, B., Vermilyea, J., & Blanchard, E. (1986). Comorbidity and depression among the anxiety disorders: Issues in diagnosis and classification. *Journal of Nervous and Mental Disorders, 174,* 63–72.

Beck, A. (1963). Thinking and depression: 2, theory and therapy. *Archives of General Psychiatry, 10,* 561–571.

Beck, A. (1976). *Cognitive therapy and the emotional disorders.* New York: International Universities Press.

Beck, A., & Emery, G. (1985). *Anxiety disorders and phobics: A cognitive perspective.* New York: Basic Books.

Beck, A., Freeman, A., & Associates (1990). *Cognitive therapy of personality disorders.* New York: Guilford.

Beck, A., Rush, A., Shaw, B., & Emery, G. (1979). *Cognitive therapy of depression.* New York: Guilford Press.

Bem, D. (1965). An experimental analysis of self-persuasion. *Journal of Experimental Psychology, 1,* 199–218.

Benson, H. (1975). *The relaxation response.* New York: William Morrow.

Benson, H., Beary, J., & Carol, M. (1974). The relaxation response. *Psychiatry, 37,* 37–46.

Berg, I., & Miller, S. (1992). *Working with the problem drinker.* New York: Norton and Co.

Berne, E. (1961). *Transactional analysis in psychotherapy.* New York: Grove Press.

Berne, E. (1973). *What do you say after you say hello.* New York: Bantam Books.

Bibring, E. (1953). The mechanism of depression. In P. Greenacre (Ed.), *Affective disorders.* New York: International Universities Press.

Bridges, W. (1980). *Transitions: Making sense of life changes.* Menlo Park, CA: Addison-Wesley.

Burns, D. (1980). *Feeling good: The New Mood Therapy.* New York: Signet Book.

Burns, M., & Seligman, M. (1989). Explanatory style across the lifespan: Evidence for stability over 52 years. *Journal of Personality and Social Psychology, 56,* 471–477.

Candland, D. (1977). The persistent problem of emotion. In D. Candland, J. Fell, E. Keen, A. Lesow, R. Platchik, & R. Tarpy (Eds.), *Emotion.* Monterrey, CA: Brooks/Cole.

Carlson, M. (1988). *Meaning-Making.* New York: Norton and Co.

Carver, C., & Scheier, M. (1999). Optimism. In C. Snyder, *Coping: The psychology of what works* (pp. 182–204). New York: Oxford University Press.

Cautela, J. (1967). Covert sensitization. *Psychological Reports, 20,* 459–468.

Cautela, J. (1973). Covert processes and behavior modification. *Journal of Nervous and Mental Disease, 157,* 27–36.

Christoff, K., & Kelly, J. (1985). A behavioral approach to social skills training with psychiatric patients. In L. L'Abate & M. Milan, *Handbook of social skills training and research* (pp. 361–388). New York: Wiley.

Cox, T. (1979). *Stress.* Baltimore, MD: University Park Press.

Craske, M., Barlow, D., & O'Leary, T. (1992). *Mastery of your anxiety and worry.* Albany, NY: Graywind Publishing.

Deffenbacher, J., & Suinn, R. (1987). General anxiety syndrome. In L. Michelson & L. Ascher (pp. 332–361). New York: Guilford Press.

de Shazer, S. (1985). *Keys to solution in brief therapy.* New York: Norton.

de Shazer, S. (1988). *Clues: Investigating solutions in brief therapy.* New York: Norton.

de Shazer, S. (1991). *Putting differences to work.* New York: W. W. Norton.

Diamond, J. (2000). *Narrative means to sober ends.* New York: Guilford Press.

Dobson, K. (1988). *Handbook of cognitive-behavioral therapies.* New York: Guilford Press.

Dobson, K. (2001). *Handbook of cognitive behavioral therapies* (2nd ed.). New York: Guilford Press.

Dobson, K., & Block, L. (1988). Historical and philosophical bases of the cognitive behavioral therapies. In K. Dobson (Ed.), *Handbook of cognitive-behavioral therapies* (pp. 3–39). New York: Guilford Press.

Dollard, J., Doob, J., Miller, N., Mowrer, O., & Sears, R. (1939). *Frustration and aggression.* New Haven, CT: Yale University Press.

Dryden, W., & Ellis, A. (1988). In K. Dobson (Ed.), *Handbook of cognitive-behavioral therapies* (pp. 214–273). New York: Guilford Press.

D'Zurilla, T., & Goldfried, M. (1971). Problem solving and behavior modification. *Journal of Abnormal Psychology, 78,* 107–126.

D'Zurilla, T., & Nezu, A. (1982). Social problem solving in adults. In A. C. Kendal (Ed.), *Advances in cognitive-behavioral research and therapy (Vol. 1).* New York: Academic Press.

Edwards, W. (1954). The theory of decision-making. *Psychological Bulletin, 51,* 380–417.

Ellis, A. (1962). *Reason and emotion in psychotherapy.* Secaucus, NJ: Lyle Stuart.

Ellis, A. (1971). *Growth through reason.* North Hollywood, CA: Wilshire Books.

Ellis, A. (1973). *Humanistic psychotherapy: The rational-emotive approach.* New York: McGraw-Hill.

Ellis, A. (1977). *Anger: How to live with and without it.* New York: Reader's Digest Press.

Ellis, A. (1979). Discomfort anxiety: A new cognitive behavioral construct. Part I. *Rational Living, 14*(2), 3–8.

Ellis, A. (1985). *Overcoming resistance.* New York: Springer.

Ellis, A., & Abrams, M. (1994). *How to cope with a fatal illness.* New York: Barricade Books.

Ellis, A., & Grieger, R. (Eds.). *Handbook of rational emotive therapy.* New York: Springer.

Ellis, A., & Harper, R. (1975). *A new guide to rational living.* North Hollywood, CA: Wilshire Books.

Ellis, A., McInerney, J. F., DiGiuseppe, R., & Yeager, R. J. (1988). *Rational-emotive therapy with alcoholics and substance abusers.* New York: Pergamon Press.

Ellis, A., & MacLaren, C. (1998). *Rational emotive behavioral therapy.* San Luis Obispo, CA: Impact Publishing

Fennell, P. (2001). *Chronic illness workbook.* Oakland, CA: New Harbinger Publishing.

Fisher, R. (1991). *Getting to Yes: Negotiating agreement without giving in* (2nd ed.). New York: Viking Press.

Fordyce, W. (1976). *Behavioral methods for chronic pain and illness.* St Louis: Mosby.

Forman, S. (1995). *Coping skills interventions for children and adolescents.* San Francisco: Jossey-Bass.

Frank, J. (1974). *Persuasion and healing.* New York: Schocken Books.

Frankl, V. (1965). *The doctor and the soul: From psychotherapy to logotherapy.* New York: Beacon Press.

Galassi, J., Galossi, M., & Vedder, M. (1981). Perspectives on assertion as a social skills model. In J. Wine & M. Smye (Eds.), *Social competence* (pp. 287–346). New York: Guilford Press.

Geer, J., Davison, G., & Gatchel, R. (1970). Reduction of stress in humans through nonverdical perceived control of aversive stimulation. *Journal of Personality and Social Psychology, 16,* 731–738.

Goldfried, M., & Davidson, G. (1976). *Clinical behavior therapy.* New York: Holt, Rinehart, & Winston.

Goldfried, M. (1980). Psychotherapy as coping skills training. In M. Mahoney (Ed.), *Psychotherapy process: Current issues and future directions* (pp. 89–121). New York: Plenum.

Goldfried, M., & Merbaum, M. (1973). *Behavior change through self-control.* New York: Holt, Rinehart, & Winston.

Gordon, D. (1978). *Therapeutic metaphors.* Phoenix: Meta Pub.

Gordon, D., & Meyers-Anderson, M. (1981). Phoenix: Meta Pub.

Gordon, T. (1970). *P.E.T: Parent effectiveness training.* New York: Wyden.

Gordon, T. (1976). *P.E.T. in action.* New York: Bantam Books.

Gorton, B. (1959). Autogenic training. *American Journal of Clinical Hypnosis, 2,* 31–41.

Greenberg, L., & Safran, J. (1987). *Emotion in psychotherapy: Affect, cognition, and the process of change.* New York: Guilford Press.

Guerney, B. (1977). *Relationship enhancement: Skills program for therapy, problem prevention, and enrichment.* San Francisco: Jossey-Bass.

Guidano, V. (1988). A systems, process-oriented approach to cognitive therapy. In K. Dobson (Ed.), *Handbook of cognitive-behavioral therapies* (pp. 307–357). New York: Guilford Press.

Haley, J. (1967). *Advanced techniques of hypnosis and therapy.* New York: Grune and Stratton.

Haley, J. (1973). *Uncommon therapy.* New York: Norton.

Haley, J. (1976). *Problem solving therapy.* San Francisco: Jossey-Bass.

Haley, J. (1984). *Ordeal therapy.* San Francisco: Jossey-Bass.

Haley, J. (1987). *Problem solving therapy, 2nd ed.* San Francisco: Jossey-Bass.

Hamilton, V. (1982). Cognition and stress: An information processing model. In L. Goldberger & S. Brenitz (Eds.), *Handbook of stress: Theoretical and clinical aspects.* New York: Free Press.

Harris, T. (1967). *I'm OK—you're OK.* New York: Harper & Row.

Heidegger, M. (1955). *What is philosophy.* New Haven: College and University Press.

Homans, G. (1967). *Nature of social science.* New York: Harcourt, Brace, and World.

Homans, G. (1974). *Social behavior: Its elementary forms.* New York: Harcourt Brace Javanovich.

Husserl, E. (1970). *The idea of phenomenology.* The Hague: Martinus Nijhoff.

Hycner, R. (1985). Dialogical Gestalt therapy: An initial proposal. *Gestalt Journal,* pp. 23–49.

Jacobson, E. (1938). *Progressive relaxation* (2nd ed.). Chicago: Chicago Press.

Jacobson, E. (1971). *Depression.* New York: International Universities Press.

Jacobson, E. (1972). *You must relax* (4th ed.). New York: McGraw-Hill.

Kanfer, F. (1970). Self-regulation: Research issues and speculations. In C. Neuringer & L. Michael (Eds.), *Behavior modification in clinical psychology.* New York: Appleton-Century-Crofts.

Kanfer, F. (1971). The maintenance of behavior by self-generated stimuli and reinforcement. In A. Jacobs & L. Sachs (Eds.), *The psychology of private events: Perspectives on covert response systems.* New York: Academic Press.

Kazdin, A. (1978). The application of operant techniques in treatment, rehabilitation, and education. In S. Garfield & A. Bergin, *Handbook of psychology and behavior change* (pp. 549–591). New York: Wiley.

Kelly, J. (1982). *Social skills training: A practical guide for interventions.* New York: Springer.

Kendall, P., & Hollon, S. (1979). *Cognitive-behavioral interventions* (pp. 11–32). New York: Academic Press.

King, M., Novik, L., & Citrenbaum, C. (1983). *Irresistible communication.* Philadelphia: Saunders.

Koffka, K. (1935). *Principles of Gestalt psychology.* New York: Harcourt, Brace & World.

Kohler, W. (1947). *Gestalt psychology.* New York: Liveright Pub. Corp.

L'Abate, L., & Milan, M. (Eds.). (1985). *Handbook of social skills training and research.* New York: Wiley and Sons.

Lazarus, A. (1968). Learning theory and the treatment of depression. *Behavior Research and Therapy, 6,* 83–89.

Luria, A. (1961). *The role of speech in the regulation of normal and abnormal behaviors.* New York: Liveright.

Mahoney, M. (1974). *Cognition and behavior modification.* Cambridge, MA: Ballinger.

Mahoney, M. (1977). Personal science: A cognitive learning therapy. In A. Ellis & R. Grieger (Eds.), *Handbook of rational psychotherapy.* New York: Springer.

Mahoney, M. (1988). The cognitive sciences and psychotherapy: Patterns in a developing relationship. In K. Dobson (Ed.), *Handbook of cognitive-behavioral therapies* (pp. 357–387). New York: Guilford Press.

Mahoney, M. & Arnkoff, D. (1978). Cognition and self-control therapies. In S. Garfield & A. Bergin (Eds.), *Handbook of psychotherapy and behavior change* (pp. 689–723). New York: Wiley.

Mahoney, M. Thoreson. (1974). *Self-control: Power to the person.* Monterey, CA: Brooks/Cole.

Marks, I. (1978). Behavioral psychotherapy of adult neuroses. In S. Garfield & A. Bergin (Eds.), *Handbook of psychotherapy and behavior change* (pp. 493–549).

Marlatt, G. (1985). Relapse prevention: Theoretical rationale and overview of the model. In G. Marlatt & J. Gordon, *Relapse prevention* (pp. 3–71). New York: Guilford Press.

Martin, T., & Doko, K. (2000). *Men don't cry . . . women do: Transcending gender stereotypes of grief.* New York: Brunner/Routledge.

Maslow, A. (1954). *Motivation and personality.* New York: Harper and Row.

Maslow, A. (1962). *Toward a psychology of being.* Princeton, NJ: van Nostrand.

May, R. (Ed.). (1961). *Existential psychology.* New York: Random House.

McMullin, K. (1986). *Handbook of cognitive therapy techniques.* New York: Norton Co.

Meichenbaum, D. (1977). *Cognitive-behavior modification: An integrated approach.* New York: Plenum.

Meichenbaum, D. (1985). *Stress inoculation training.* New York: Pergamon Press.

Meichenbaum, D., & Jaremko, M. (1983). *Stress reduction and prevention.* New York: Plenum.

Melzack, R., & Wall, P. (1965). Pain mechanisms: A new theory. *Science, 1965, 50,* 971–979.

Melzack, R., & Wall, P. (1970). Psychology of pain. *International Anesthesiology Clinic, 8,* 3–34.

Milan, M., & Kolko, D. (1985). Social skills training and complementary strategies in anger control and the treatment of aggressive behavior. In L. L'Abate & M. Milan (Eds.), *Handbook of social skills training and research* (pp. 101–136). New York: Wiley.

Naranjo, C. (1980). *The techniques of Gestalt therapy.* Highland, NY: Gestalt Journal.

Navaco, R. (1975). *Anger control: The development and evaluation of experimental treatment.* Lexington, MA: Heath and Co.

O'Hanlon. W. (1987). *Taproots.* New York: Norton.

O'Hanlan, W., & Weiner, M. (1989). *In search of solutions: A new direction in psychotherapy.* New York: Norton.

Osborn, A. (1963). *Applied imagination: Principles and procedures of creative problem solving* (3rd ed.). New York: Scribner.

Pelletier, K. (1977). *Mind as healer, mind as slayer.* New York: Dell Publishing.

Perls, F. (1966). *Ego, hunger, and aggression.* San Francisco: Orbit-Esalen.

Perls, F. (1972). *In and out the garbage pail.* New York: Bantam Books.

Perls, F., Hefferline, R., & Goodman, P. (1951). *Gestalt therapy.* New York: Julian Press.

Pittman, F. (1987). *Turning points.* New York: Norton.

Poppen, R. (1988). *Behavioral relaxation training and assessment.* New York: Pergamon Press.

Polster, E., & Polster, M. (1973). *Gestalt therapy integrated.* New York: Vintage Books.

Rehm, L., & Rokhe, P. (1988). Self-management therapies. In K. Dobson, *Handbook of cognitive behavior therapies* (pp. 136–166). New York: Guilford Press.

Rice, L., & Greenberg, L. (1991). Two affective change events in client-centered therapy. In J. Safran & L. Greenberg (Eds.), *Emotion, psychotherapy, and change.* New York: Guilford Press.

Rogers, C. (1961). *On becoming a person.* Boston: Houghton Mifflin.

Rosch, E. (1973). Natural categories. *Cognitive Psychology, 4,* 328–350.

Rosch, E. (1975). Cognitive representations of semantic categories. *Journal of Experimental Psychology: General, 104,* 192–233.

Rosch, E., & Mervis, C. (1975). Family resemblances: Studies in the international structure of categories. *Cognitive Psychology, 7,* 573–605.

Rosch, E., Mervis, C., Gray, W., Johnson, D., & Boyes-Braem, P. (1976). Basic objects in natural categories. *Cognitive Psychology, 8,* 382–439.

Salkovskis, P. (1996). *Frontiers of cognitive therapy.* New York: Guilford.

Schultz, J., & Luthe, W. (1969). *Autogenic training (vol. 1).* New York: Grune and Stratton.

Scott, D., & Barber, T. (1977). Cognitive control of pain: Effects of multiple cognitive strategies. *Psychological Record, 27,* 373–383.

Selekman, M. (1999). *Pathways to change: Brief therapy solutions with difficult adolescents.* New York: Guilford Press.

Seligman, M. (1975). *Helplessness: On depression, development and death.* San Francisco: Freeman.

Seligman, M., & Maier, S. (1967). Failure to escape traumatic shock. *Journal of Experimental Psychology, 63,* 23–33.

Seltzer, L. (1986). *Paradoxical strategies in psychotherapy.* New York: Wiley and Sons.

Selye, H. (1976). *Stress of life.* New York: McGraw-Hill.

Sharoff, K. (2002). *Cognitive coping therapy.* New York: Brunner/Routledge.

Shatte, A., Reivich, K., Gillham, J., & Seligman, M. (1999). Learned optimism in children. In C. Snyder (Ed.), *Coping.* New York: Oxford University Press.

Sheikh, A. (1983). *Imagery: Current theory, research, and application.* New York: Wiley and Sons.

Shure, M. (1981). Social competence as a problem solving skill. In M. Smye & J. Wine (Eds.), *Social competence.* New York: Guilford Press.

Snyder, C., Cheavens, J., & Michael, S. (1999). Hoping. In C. Snyder (Ed.), *Coping: The psychology of what works* (pp. 205–231). New York: Oxford University Press.

Snyder, C., & Dinoff, B. (1999). Coping: Where have you been? In C. Snyder, *Coping: The psychology of what works* (pp. 3–20). New York: Oxford University Press.

Spivack, G., Platt, J., & Shure, M. (1976). *The problem-solving approach to adjustment.* San Francisco: Jossey-Bass.

Sprafkin, R., Gershaw, N., & Goldstein, A. (1993). *Social skills for mental health.* Boston: Allyn & Bacon.

Sternbach, R. (1998). Treatment of the chronic pain patient. *Journal of Human Stress, 4,* 11–15.

Sternbach, R., & Rusk, T. (1973). Alternatives to the pain career. *Psychotherapy: Theory, Research, and Practice, 10,* 321–324.

Suinn, R. (1976). Anxiety management training to control general anxiety. In J. Krumbolta & C. Thoresen (Eds.), *Counseling methods.* New York: Holt, Rinehart, Winston.

Turk, D., Meichenbaum, D., & Genest, M. (1983). *Pain and behavioral medicine: A cognitive behavioral perspective.* New York: Guilford Press.

Van De Riet, V., Korb, M., & Gorrell, J. (1980). *Gestalt therapy: An introduction.* New York: Pergamon Press.

Vygotsky, L. (1962). *Thought and language.* New York: Wiley.

Wackman, D., & Wampler, K. (1985). The couple communication program. In L. L'Abate & M. Milan, *Handbook of social skills training and research.* New York: Wiley.

Watts, A. (1965). *The way of Zen.* New York: Random House.

Watzlawick, P., Weakland, J., & Fisch, R. (1974). *Change.* New York: Norton.

Weeks, G., & L'Abate, L. (1982). *Paradoxical psychotherapy: Theory and practice with individuals, couples, and families.* New York: Brunner/Mazel.

Wessler, R., & Wessler, R. (1980). *The principles and practice of rational-emotive therapy.* San Francisco: Jossey-Bass.

Wine, J. (1981). From defect to competence models. In J. Wine & M. Smye (Eds.), *Social competence* (pp. 3–36). New York: Guilford Press.

Wine, J., & Smye, M. (1981). *Social competence.* New York: Guilford Press.

Wolpe, J. (1958). *Psychotherapy by reciprocal inhibition.* Stanford, CA: Stanford University Press.

Wolpe, J. (1969). *The practice of behavior therapy.* Oxford: Pergamon.

Wolpe, J. (1973). *The practice of behavior therapy* (2nd ed.). New York: Pergamon Press.

Zeig, J. (Ed.). (1980). *A teaching seminar with Milton H. Erickson.* New York: Brunner/Mazel.

Zinker, J. (1977). *Creative process in Gestalt therapy.* New York: Brunner/Mazel.

Index

Springer Publishing Company

Stress Management

A Comprehensive Handbook of Techniques and Strategies

Jonathan C. Smith, PhD

"...a state-of-the-art book...practical methods of treatment for those who need help managing stress in their lives...ideal as a graduate level text or resource..."

—**Martin Weinstein**, PhD, Associate Professor Roosevelt University, School of Psychology

"...an invaluable tool in educating both undergraduate and graduate students, in psychology and across disciplines...clinicians and their clients would be hard-pressed to find a more useful text..."

—**Dena Traylor**, PsyD, Roosevelt University

This clinical manual contains detailed descriptions of tactics for training the user in the methods of relaxation, positive thinking, time management, and more. Features validated self-tests (normed on over 1000 individuals), and first-time-ever stress management motivations and irrational beliefs inventories.

Partial Contents:

Part I. Stress Basics • Stress Competency and the Smith Stress Management Skills Inventory • Stress Concepts, Exercises

Part II. The Four Pillars of Stress Management • Progressive Muscle Relaxation and Autogenic Training • Breathing and Stretching Exercises • Sense Imagery and Meditation • Relaxation, Centering, and Stress Management Exercises • Identifying Clear and Concrete Problem Cues • Stress Inoculation and Relapse Prevention

Part III. Interpersonal Skills: Relationships and Stress Management • Assertiveness, Exercises • Empathy and Assertive Coping • Goals and Priorities • Relaxation Beliefs, Active Coping Beliefs, and Philosophy of Life

2002   280pp   0-8261-4947-2   hardcover

536 Broadway, New York, NY 10012 • **Order Toll-Free: 877-687-7476**
Fax: 212-941-7842 • **Order On-line: www.springerpub.com**